AF421974

Praise for Memoirs of an American Buddhist in Los Angeles

Loved her storytelling of synchronicity infused with genuine authenticity and humor! Couldn't put it down! What an amazing life! I can't wait to see what's next!

— Jeffrey Acidera, Adjunct Academic Counselor, College of the Desert

Charmingly written! The author reveals the simultaneous occurrence of events comprising reality as she journals through her life. She gives us a crack in the door peek as she shares the perspective of her Buddhist awareness and the life she comes to love. Compiling the past, present, and future, and revelations, patterns emerge that once remained unseen.

— Toni Arinsberg, Photographer

Deborah shares her stories, truths, and experiences in a simple yet eloquent way with clarity, love, and a dash of humor. I thank her for inspiring my return to the "practice."

— Diane Moss, Music Therapist

Intriguing connections, amazing timing, reflections of the richness of being human; Memoirs of An American Buddhist in Los Angeles captured my full attention. It delighted and inspired me. Deborah's examples of moving her life into victory through chanting Nam-myoho-renge-kyo are astonishing. In a time of such great chaos and negativity, this read filled my heart with joy and hope for my personal challenges and for all of humanity.

— Lydia Darby, Healing Facilitator

I thoroughly enjoyed the candid description of Deborah's experiences. Each page kept me wanting to get to the next page. The synchronistic events in her life were nothing less than miraculous. The influence of Buddhism clearly added a richness to her life. Deborah's story will surely inspire readers to pay attention to the coincidences that lead to surprises that one never expects.

— Alice Bartlett, Psychotherapist

Memoirs of An American Buddhist in Los Angeles reminds me of my own struggles and obstacles. After reading this book, I was moved to look inward and decided to try this Buddhist practice where I have found endless inspiration and compassion.

— Violette Belle

Congratulations to the author on this challenging endeavor! I think it took a lot of courage to open her personal life to bring people in. I particularly enjoyed her creative way of explaining Buddhist basics and found the widespread range of her testimonials, as they related to the relationships in her life, to be inspiring.

— **Victoria Evans,** Poet, Writer, Life Coach, Public Speaker

Memoirs of an American Buddhist in Los Angeles is filled with gut-wrenching, soul-searching courage and grit. The complexities of Deborah's life take on poignancy and drama through her own eyes and her engaging dialogue. Her honesty in sharing her entire history is remarkable. Deborah has achieved a great deal of wisdom and personal transformation through self-reflection and personal responsibility to change the trajectory of her life into a valuable example of victory through her practice of Buddhism.

— **Eileen Lion**

As a practicing SGI-USA Buddhist, I can't help but feel awestruck with a greater understanding and inspiration. Deborah breathes a freshness and determination to the human soul that no matter how dire, to absolutely win resolutely! Thank you for allowing me to read your life's journey. It was a beautiful roller coaster ride and many treasures of inspiration!

— **Angela Nix,** News Journalist

This author proves synchronicity through her own life experience. An interesting story that weaves the interconnectedness of many people through different time periods and places. I really enjoyed reading this book!

—**Carmen Thielemann,** Author

After reading Deborah's book, I thought, "I want to be like her when I grow up," and then I remembered… no, I want to be the best me! That's what she wants you to know... to learn to be the best you! Enjoy!

— **Sylvia Ruiz-Lee,** Domestic Diva

Favorite cleverly shares with us her early years of an undeniable profound thirst for acceptance to nullify a life fraught with rejection, tragedy, loneliness, and vengeance. As a reader, it's moving to be able to experience her life's fluctuations and to see how she flourishes and finds fulfillment once she starts to carry out a Buddhist lifestyle. Her thirst is quenched through such strong acceptance and enrichment of herself that it becomes an enlightenment to people around her. As does this book!

—**Jinyoung Noh,** Retired Business Owner

I was amazed by the bravery of the author's storytelling! She reminds us of what it means to be human, to find the courage to connect with what is best about our lives!

—**Jesse Nelson James,** Instructor of Sign Language

What a pleasure it was to read this memoir. I couldn't help but feel the pain of her childhood, and I was moved by her WOW moments after chanting and the happy endings to so many critical circumstances. Her ups and downs describe life as it really is. This was an easy read and I encourage everyone to pick it up. Very enjoyable!

— **Roxie Patterson,** VP of Antelope Valley Unitarian Universalist Fellowship; Community Activist

It's definitely no coincidence, but a gift of synchronicity, that Memoirs found its way to me. Deborah's life experiences are often jaw-dropping, frequently relatable, but most of all, important lessons about the gifts our coexistence holds if you're open to receive them. Open your mind, open your heart and dive in, it's a wild ride!

— **Sister Roma,** Sisters of Perpetual Indulgence, San Francisco

Favorite shows us through example after example that our own lives can also experience synchronicity if only we are open to receiving it.

— **Laura Aved,** Editor

Memoirs of an American Buddhist in Los Angeles

Synchronicity is No Coincidence

Memoirs of an American Buddhist in Los Angeles is a memoir. No names have been changed, no characters invented, no events fabricated. Although I have been corrected on some points… primarily speling, and gramer, I have done my very best to tell it like it was.

Library of Congress

synchronicityisnocoincidence.com

Cover design by Kai Hill

Dedicated to
my BFF, No. 1 Cheerleader
& MMM (Most Magnificent Muse)
AuntieToni

APPRECIATION

This section is so much more than an acknowledgment— this is my deepest, most heartfelt expression of appreciation!

To my mom: thank you for allowing me the time I needed to break through my shackles and grow exponentially because of our trauma and drama. You held the original spirit to NEVER GIVE UP!

To my fathers: the one who gave me life but didn't have the courage to participate in it; and to the one who raised me in the best way he could despite his own pain.

To my daughter and my son: you are my shining stars. You have developed into smart, compassionate, stellar humans and I love you more than I can express.

To my three amazing grandsons: you are champions in the art of overcoming the odds.

To my sisters: you have been my role models, each in your own unique way.

To my grandparents, my many aunties, uncles, oodles of cousins, nieces, and nephews: you have been, and will continue to be, the heirloom of legacy-creators for our jumbo-sized family.

To my dear friends and SGI family: you have been my rock-solid support through thick and thin, tears and laughter, and who have inspired and encouraged me to stretch my boundaries beyond comprehension.

To all the horn honkers: you helped me unleash an important side of my humanity.

To my Cuzin Diane: you introduced me, albeit kicking and screaming, to this phenomenal Buddhist practice that has opened my life to all its infinite miracles.

To my mentor, Daisaku Ikeda: your unparalleled example of how to live as a human being is forever branded in my heart!

MY HUMAN REVOLUTION

The path I have chosen to walk upon has many crossroads from previous travels,
As does the mighty oak with its countless blossoming branches,
To tell the tales of its life's growth.

If I could share my pain with you,
        The tears of loss, the cries of defeat,
        The anger gouging at my innermost life force,
But never quitting!

They were and are the tears of loss…
        But never losing.
They were and are the tears of defeat…
        But never being defeated.
The anger was, and is, welling up from my innermost life force,
        And it was, and is, the pattern for my growth.
The loss, the defeat, the anger…
Are minute steppingstones along this path I have chosen to walk upon.

If I could share my joy with you,
        The tears of happiness, the cries of laughter,
        The overwhelming sensations of my innermost life force,
Always forging ahead!

They were, and are, the tears of happiness…
        And always searching.
They were, and are, the cries of laughter…
        And always sincere.
It was, and is, the overwhelming sensations of my innermost life force,
        And realizing there is so much more!

If I could share my life with you,
        The challenge of my mission,
        The reality of life's scattered puzzle concealing the answers,
        The struggle of finding pieces that fit,
        The indefinable encouragement conceived from the love of friends,
Developing in a burning sensation to touch your life with mine…
        Is the purpose of my Human Revolution!

TABLE OF CONTENTS

FOUR–WORDS

INTRODUCTION 1

THE BEGINNING

1 Welcome to My Life 7

2 Sneak Preview 13

3 My First Marriage 16

THE MIDDLE

4 An American Buddhist in Los Angeles 21

5 My First Buddhist Meeting 24

6 The Hawaii Convention 26

7 My Second Buddhist Meeting 28

8 The Parking Meter 31

9 Literal Translation No.1 33

10 The Man in the Urology Department 37

11 Literal Translation No.2 39

12 The Pap Smear 42

13 The Sunshine of My Life 44

14 Stanley Avenue 58

15 Becoming A Mommy 61

16 Too Close for Comfort 66

17 Donna and Dr. Weinstein 70

18 The Tree of Life 73

19 Ischemic Colitis 77

20 Nana and the Fairytale Warrior 82

21 The Trial 88

22 Guardian Angels 95

THE PRESENT

23 Epilogue: Falling in Love...*With Me*   113

PUDDLEJUMPERS

The Kiss   125

Judy, Judy, Judy   127

Mrs. Beasley   129

Grammy Award Winner   130

Return to Camelot   130

Oh, How Lively   131

Melody... Music to My Ears   133

Instant Message   134

Online Dating   134

Ellen and the Elevator   136

AFTER-WORDS   140

Thirst Quenchers

Audio Visual

For More Info

FOUR-WORDS

Courage /kerij/noun: the ability to do something that frightens one; strength in the face of pain or grief.

Determination /determenāSH(e)n/noun: firmness of purpose; resoluteness.

Compassion /kempaSHen/noun: sympathetic consciousness of others' distress together with a desire to alleviate it.

Victory /vikt(e)rē/noun: achievement of mastery or success in a struggle or endeavor against odds or difficulties.

"There are more things
In heaven and earth, Horatio
Than are dreamt of in your philosophy."
—Shakespeare

INTRODUCTION

Over my lifetime, I have learned to pay attention to the profound guidance my surroundings so freely avail. When I allow myself to carefully listen, I am most assuredly bestowed with the synchronistic benefits of life-altering gifts... gifts chock-full with magic and wonder. For many years I have kept a running log documenting these mind-boggling events. Until recently, I believed that my synchronistic stories somehow separated me from the norm. But as I've continued my journey, I am discovering that this special endowment I have is there for all to tap into... it is simply a matter of taking the time to listen and pay attention.

One afternoon, not too long ago, while walking with two co-workers in the court-yard of the building I worked in, we passed an ATM. The machine was making a rather loud and alarming mechanical noise, and although I heard the noise, and in my mind acknowledged it, I subconsciously chose to put it aside and continued with our conversation.

One of the women I was talking with declared in jest, "Someone get me a bucket, I think that puppy is about to pay off!" She was in tune with that potential opportunity should it decide to knock. I was the one who, having also heard the noise, chose to ignore it and the potential opportunity of a big payoff. A third possibility might be that some other individual happening upon that ATM at the same time we did, may have halted in defeat assuming the machine had run dry just when they desperately needed a withdrawal.

Each of us has our own sense of reality. Is the glass half empty or half full? I imagine the answer depends upon our needs at the time, and of course, whether or not we are paying attention.

I believe certain circumstances sometimes present themselves as life lessons. And, again, if we aren't paying attention, chances are the same circumstances will present themselves until we do.

An example of this scenario would be one of my many life lessons. For years, it seemed that EVERY TIME I was behind the wheel of my car, whether I was driving on a main thoroughfare, on the freeway, in a residential neighborhood, or waiting at a red light — there would inevitably be a car behind me honking with obnoxious persistence. I can't count how many times the light had not even changed from red to green before the car behind me was honking. Eventually, I began rolling down my window and signaling for the jerk to go around. Also, EVERY SINGLE TIME this occurred, my get nasty back button was triggered, and I responded in kind, "What the f - - - do you want me to do a - - - - - -!"

One day, as I attempted to make a right-hand turn, pedestrians stepped off the curb to cross the street. The person in the car behind me laid on his horn. Just as I was about to get out of my car and give him a piece of my mind, a thought came to me... *I wonder what happened to him today. Maybe he's late to work because his child is sick and if he's late one more time, he'll lose his job... or, maybe he just got a call that his wife had been in an accident and was rushing to the emergency room.* This became a vital realization to my own awakening. It was a portal. Since that day, it has been a rare occasion to have someone honking behind me. On that rare occasion, my first thought is to question what may be happening to that person, and I graciously move out of their way.

I have come to believe that all of us have the potential to realize multitudes of opportunities but, oftentimes, we're either asleep when opportunity knocks, or we're at the airport when our ship comes in. Whatever the reasons for our personal lack of magic or rhythm, we choose not to see or hear what surrounds us. We close our lives off from the experience of living. We close ourselves off from our own miracles and good fortune by not paying attention to the universe surrounding our lives and all that it might have to offer. I believe miracles encircle us at every moment, but it is our responsibility to tap into them, to open ourselves up, and become our own dream catchers.

Someone once told me a story of a woman who held a small bird cupped in her hands. When the woman opened her hands to let the bird go, it took the bird a full minute before it moved or spread its wings… the bird didn't realize it was free. When I examine my own invisible shackles, I come to see and understand how deep the limitations are that I place on my own existence. Giving myself permission to open my wings to fly toward a goal oftentimes becomes a debilitating maneuver in and of itself. I believe when I choke off my own breath of life, miracles cannot find their way to me. That does not mean they are not hovering all around awaiting my effort to open the door of the gilded cage and let my wings take flight.

We all experience fears… especially the fear of moving into uncharted waters. But before we can fly, we must encounter wind resistance to lift us up. And, before we can soar, we must break through a veritable wall. It all boils down to choices — our choices. Have you ever experienced that sensational empowerment once you've summoned up the courage to blast through that wall, to win over the struggle and realize your dreams, to fight for what is rightfully yours or to right a terrible wrong? That is truly living! Those abysmal obstructions that block our way transform into mere steppingstones. Creating a shift in perception becomes the source by which we tap that power and can call upon it again and again and again. My mom used to say, "Never leave the house without your eyebrows on." I was well into my fifties when it dawned on me that what she was saying was, "Always put your best foot forward."

So, what exactly is synchronicity? The first time I heard that word was on August 13, 1998, when I attended a lecture by Carol Adrienne at the Bodhi Tree Bookstore in Los Angeles. Carol co-authored *The Celestine Vision* with James Redfield and she was there to speak about her new book, *The Purpose of Your Life*. Commonly the word synchronicity is interchanged with coincidence. However, to be "in sync" certainly does not indicate a chance happening or an accidental occurrence; it would more clearly indicate being at the right place at the right time for some remarkable occurrence of events to become manifest.

One of my most treasured childhood memories was of such magnitude it has been difficult to express in words for it was truly spiritual in nature. I grew up in the desert in Lancaster, California. I was around nine when this incredible event took place. It was summertime and I would often camp out in my sleeping bag by myself in the backyard. I would lie there for hours studying the sky. In those days, the nights were magnificent. I remember the sky, the universe, the smell of the night, the way the summer air felt on my skin, the phenomenal sunrise. We lived in a tiny community and the light factor was so low I could not see the dark for the brightness of the stars. One night as I lay watching and listening, a shooting star pierced the sky. Witnessing the event of a shooting star certainly was not a novelty. Not in those days. The vastness of what surrounded me was so clear and so great, I swear I could see the depths of it all. But that night, when that star shot by, I experienced something so profound that my entire being grasped its effect. In the flash of time that it took to burn itself out, I felt the expanse of a universal truth, one which was branded on my soul. I did not have the maturity to understand what had occurred, but I know that what I had encountered was powerful and unique to me. I have carried that moment with me always, and perhaps it's related in some cyclic, mystical way to my purpose and reason for the incredible stories I am about to share. I do know that most everyone experiences a coincidence now and again. Naturally, it's expected. But I know of few people who have had the incredible fortune to experience the profound complexity and frequency of synchronicities that land at my doorstep. They have displayed no boundaries in time or space, and I am forever awed at the deepest level of my being.

My stories and poetry were born from my own life… sparks which only come from the joys and pains of living. As we evolve, so does our compassion. I have learned that we cannot bask in the light without having been encased in darkness. They are opposite sides of the same coin. They coexist. They complement each other. They lend a sense of harmony and balance to our existence.

This compilation is my legacy. If I continue to pay attention and carefully listen, new life experiences filled with magic and awe will emerge and touch my soul, and I will again be inspired to put pen to paper.

5

THE BEGINNING

Those who at first may be completely overwhelmed by their environment or constantly defeated by their weaknesses but who then undergo dramatic personal transformation as a result of solid Buddhist practice can be wonderful inspirations for others. The most intense suffering, unbearable agony and seemingly insurmountable deadlock are actually brilliant opportunities for doing our human revolution.

Daisaku Ikeda

1

WELCOME
TO
MY LIFE

Why, may you ask? Well, as of April 2019, the Earth was populated with 7.7 billion humanoids… give or take. It is unfathomable to imagine that no two snow-flakes are alike, right? And, just as unfathomable is to imagine that the same phenomenon applies to homo sapiens as well. With that in mind, scientifically speaking, there are 7.7 billion unique and wonderful stories to be told. Naturally, many share similarities in their drama and comedy, but nevertheless, they remain distinct.

The vim and vigor of my new life was thrust into this world at 11:33 a.m. in Santa Monica, California on Christmas Eve of 1949. Capricorn sun. Pisces moon *and* rising. My new life will be ripe as a deeply sensitive empath, a visionary, a dreamer. My new life will be ripe as a surefooted climber, although many years will pass before these two elements merge and unite in harmony. Until then, havoc will rule.

Fumbling through the mental chronicles of my childhood, the imagery in my mind's eye plants me right smack in the middle of a Norman Rockwell painting. For an innocent, imbedding oneself within such a canvas would undeniably provide a blanket of security, but in the real dimension of this world, my life was not portrayed in that canvas, and I suppose neither is anyone else's. But, as the wish-filled coins were tossed into the well with every drop of hope that I might magically step inside that frame, the coins inevitably drifted to the bottom.

Despite the perpetual sorrow that consumed my family, even as a young child I sensed a hidden place deep within that always fell short of any reasonable description or explanation. It was a rhythm… a sound… a knowing.

I was about a year old when my mom and dad divorced. I have no recollection of my father, George. Mom told me that one evening when I was an infant we had gone to dinner at my grandparents' home (George's parents). His parents immigrated from Greece when George was a baby. Mom said that when we sat down at the table, my grandfather made it quite clear that he did not want Jews in his house. And that, as they say, was that.

Mom and I went to live with her parents on Dudley Avenue in Venice Beach. We were literally just steps from the boardwalk and the sand. In those days, that's where the poor people lived. Go figure! We were a crowded bunch: my grandparents, my mom, my Auntie Gogi, my cousin Jeri, my Uncle Norman, Auntie Nikki (both teenagers), and me.

At bedtime, I was put in my crib with the door shut behind. I remember feeling a presence lurking in the darkness. I saw pinwheels coming at me and I screamed myself to sleep every night. To this day, I sleep with the bedroom door open and a night light to guide me.

When I was four, my mom married Don. They took me to a big courthouse to meet a judge who wore a daunting black robe, but he had a nice face. I sat in a big leather chair with my little feet in new patent leather shoes and lacy socks dangling over the side. I remember the judge asking me how I felt about Don becoming my new daddy. I had no idea what any of that meant since I had never had one of those. After shrugging my shoulders, they told me, "You have one now."

I suffered from asthma, and it was advised that we leave the ocean air and move to a dry climate. Off we went — small town USA — Lancaster, California — into a country house that was named "the Old Rankin Place." We lived there until our new house was finished being constructed. The Old Rankin Place was just like a house the settlers built when they moved out west. There was a cratered duck pond at the base of a little hill surrounded by large shade trees. The highlight of my days was climbing up and down the hill to chase and feed the ducks. The faucet in the kitchen sink was a pump handle. That's where I took my bath… in the kitchen sink. After a while, we moved into our new home.

At the end of our street, the desert stretched for as far as you could see. Exploring winding pathways that circled around tumbleweeds and Joshua trees, I discovered mysterious treasures. Fool's Gold was one of them. Oh, how I loved the way it would sparkle and shine when the light hit it. One time, I brought home a cow's skull, which unearthed my childhood curiosity of becoming an archeologist. Excavating that skull was as grand as discovering the Lost City of Atlantis… whatever that might be. My mom promptly threw it away. I rarely understood grownups.

Early on, music became an integral part of my great escape. Mom always had music playing… Montovani, Johnny Mathis, Ella Fitzgerald, Nancy Wilson, Della Reese, Nat King Cole… and Gogi Grant. At five years old, I'd sneak into mom's closet and slip into her skirts and high heels and play her records. I'd close my eyes and Montovani would carry me to another time and place where I would dance in imaginary moonlight. In my mind's eye, I transformed into a beautiful young woman with long dark hair rhythmically blowing in the breeze with the dancing wheat. Off in the distance stood a handsome young man. In slow motion, we would bound across the field into each other's arms.

On February 9, 1955, my sister Nancy was born. What a beauty she was with tons of dark hair and big hazel eyes. Mom would prop her up in my arms so I could feed her. The best part about that was holding her over my shoulder and patting her little back until she let out a walloping burp. What a great thing!

My sister Donna followed on March 21, 1956, the First Day of Spring. Her appearance was coupled with a condition called celiac disease. At that time, not much was known about it. What they did know was that her tiny body was unable to absorb her food, and malnutrition set in.

In early June of the same year, a terrible thing happened that would be a life-changer for us all. Donna was only three months old when she suffered her first dreadful celiac attack. The closest hospital was 25 miles away. The day before, my mom had had extensive oral surgery and she was heavily medicated for pain. None of our neighbor friends were around and my dad was out of town on business. Mom had no choice but to pack up her babies and drive to the hospital. I was six years old. And I was in school.

My mom, Nancy and Donna didn't come home that day… or the next… or the next.

There were no freeways back then, and the road from Lancaster to Kaiser Hospital in Panorama City was through the mountains with a modest amount of civilization in between.

Mom passed out at the wheel. No other cars were involved… just a mountain.

As I walked home from school a couple of days later, one of my classmates, Richard, was circling me teasing and laughing and saying things that made me so scared. He said my mom and sisters had been killed in a car accident. He seemed to think that was pretty funny stuff. But it made my heart hurt to the depths of my being. I couldn't breathe.

I had been staying with one of our neighbors, Bobbie. I told her what Richard said and she started to cry. She hugged me tight and told me I would be okay. She didn't tell me when my mom and sisters were coming home. I thought it might be a long, long time.

After a few days, I had to leave Bobbie's and go to some stranger's house to sleep for a couple of nights. And then I had to go someplace else and then someplace else. All I knew was that I had a terrible knot in my stomach that wasn't going away. I just wanted to go home. Why did they abandon me?

I was afraid to go to sleep because I had nightmares every night. I dreamt I was walking in our neighborhood and then suddenly everything looked foreign. I was lost. I could never find my way home. Sometimes I dreamt that kids down the street would corral me into their backyard in the dark of night and stab me with swords and lick the blood. I could physically feel the pain of the stabbings, and I couldn't escape. I frequently dreamt I was a young child, maybe three or four years old, standing in a pile of rubble crying for my mommy. There was bombing all around me as an ominous blimp slowly rose from behind. I would wake with a start. I had never seen a blimp before. I had no knowledge of war. Not in this lifetime anyway. I had dreams of vicious monster-like adults chasing me through the streets, my breathing becoming incredibly labored as I ran from them. Just when they were on my heels and about to grab me, I was able to fly above their heads, but the energy it took flapping my arms was more than I could bear. The telephone wires above my head crisscrossed into a mesh prohibiting me from flying through it. It was exhausting and my breathing became more and more labored as I struggled to stay afloat in the air.

The strangers where I stayed didn't pay much attention to me. Everyone's rules were different, and it was always apparent that I was more of a burden than anything. I remember them making me eat things I didn't like, and if I cried in the night, they just told me to hush. I don't remember much besides that, except for the nightmares. I remember the nightmares.

I found out later that my mom and sisters had been in a car accident and that Nancy was going to be different… and so was my mom.

Only one time in more than six months was I allowed to see my mom. I stood on the walkway outside her fourth-floor hospital room. It had a large sliding glass door where I could peek in. She was tied to a pole floating in suspension. Her body was wrapped in bandages, and she looked like a Halloween mummy. I thought I saw her looking at me. I think she was crying. So was I.

Donna had landed in some bushes during the accident and only suffered a few scrapes and bruises. Nancy was another story altogether. She had landed on her head on the pavement. Both retinas were severed, and she suffered brain damage, never to progress much beyond the abilities of a five-year old. She was only 18-months old at the time.

Mom's body had been badly broken, and she was told that she'd never walk again. After a long time, they all came home… mom walking with a cane. She cried all the time. Everything certainly was different. For years I lived with the guilt that I had been spared.

Daddy couldn't handle the devastation. He didn't like being at home. He began spending more and more time on the golf course at the country club with his buddies and coming home drunk most every night. His wife and children were damaged goods. Alcohol numbed the reality of his pain, I suppose. Eventually, his drinking made him cruel, and the cruelty was all directed at me… the healthy one… the one who really didn't belong to him. The only time I didn't leave the dinner table in tears, was when he wasn't home. He never laid a hand on me, but he beat me down emotionally. I think sometimes it's just as bad. My mom's sister, Auntie Joan, did what she could to convince my parents to let me live with them because of the way my dad treated me. That was simply not going to happen. Not until well into my adulthood would I come to make any sense of it all.

I cried and cried throughout my childhood for being teased and bullied about being chubby. And then Mom made an appointment to see Dr. Lask. We had never seen Dr. Lask before. Dr. Dorfleur had always been our doctor. Dr. Lask said I had a thyroid deficiency, although he never tested my blood. Meet my first drug dealer, he prescribed Dexadrine — refillable anytime — no return visit necessary. My energy was phenomenal. I lost a lot of weight and morphed into a gorgeous creature. In 1966, a book titled, *Valley of the Dolls* was published. We were only in 1962 when I lived in the Antelope Valley of the Dolls. I was 11-years old. The stage was set for a dark and scarred future.

2

SNEAK PREVIEW

My Name is Deborah… and I've been told that I'm a psychic. According to Webster's Ninth New Collegiate Dictionary, the hardbound salmon-colored one that resides just to the left of my computer, the definition of psychic is: lying outside the sphere of physical science or knowledge; sensitive to nonphysical or supernatural forces and influences, marked by extraordinary or mysterious sensitivity, perception, or understanding. The definition of a medium is: something in a middle position; an individual held to be a channel of communication between the earthly world and a world of spirits; entertainment. I don't know that I communicate with spirits, but I do know I stand in the middle of some invisible system and provide a channel or means for incredible events in the gathering and linking of people. I do possess a sensitivity to nonphysical or supernatural forces… and it certainly has been entertaining.

If you've seen *American Graffiti* or *Grease*, you will have a complete understanding of my high school experience. Byron was my big crush. He had enormous penetrating blue eyes, full sensuous lips and he stood about 5 foot, 11 inches. His shaggy, thick, sandy-colored hair always had that slightly tousled look and just enough hair fell over his eye to give him that irresistible James Dean appeal.

I remember the first time I noticed him. I was in my freshman year of high school. My English class was held in a row of temporary buildings across a huge grassy field away from the main campus. We called it The Annex. Byron's English class was right before mine, and every day we would pass each other in the field. That passing became the high point of my days… it became my purpose for going to school.

My daily morning ritual consisted of propping the album cover of *My Name is Barbra* on the bathroom counter so I could arrange my hair and make-up to unfailingly match the high drama of Streisand's. I practiced her moves, her hand gestures, her facial expressions. Once the image had been perfected, I confidently made my way to school.

I spent my field-crossing time looking everywhere for Byron, and the moment I spied his whereabouts, goosebumps surfaced, and my flip-flopping stomach could easily have won an Olympic Gold Medal in gymnastics. As he drew near, I would gear myself up for a greeting he would find irresistible. And every day, all I could muster was a casual look in the other direction.

Of course, I possessed a much smoother, sophisticated, and unprecedented bravery at home with my pillow. Our fictional conversations and kisses were scenes from the greatest romance film yet to be made, with winning imagery and brilliant dialogue. I was smart, flirtatious, and sexy. I always knew just the right thing to say, and just how to say it. Boy, could he kiss! And, oh, how I longed to feel the warmth and tenderness of lips that were not filled with down feathers pressed against mine.

Byron must have sensed my silent beckoning. The first time he knocked on my door, it was about 10:00 in the evening. I had just crawled into bed adorned in my new and most favorite flannel nightgown. It was white with small, delicate pink flowers, and was lusciously soft. The neck was ruffled, and the skirt was full. I loved the way it caressed my skin. I could smell the faded fragrance of Windsong gently lingering on my body from the morning hours.

My bedroom window was just to the right of the front door. I peeked out to see who would be knocking at such a late hour. I nearly fainted when I saw him standing on the front porch. I feared he might hear my heart beating through the walls. I quickly and quietly slipped into my bathrobe and slippers and went to the door.

We sat on the porch steps watching the chilly Fall air give form and color to our breath. It was wonderful having him there by my side. He left a while later, and

I went back to bed in a complete and total lovesick stupor. We never really had much to say… he was deeply shy. We simply enjoyed the quiet of being together.

I had lots of pajamas and nightgowns, and certainly they were alternated quite frequently. I can't imagine that I ever wore the same pair of anything twice in a row. I do know that the next time I wore that nightgown, which may have been two weeks later, Byron appeared on my doorstep at 10:00 just after I curled deep into the layer of blankets on my bed.

A week later, as I climbed into bed wearing my favorite nightgown, and before I heard the knock, I poked my nose through the curtain of my bedroom window and saw Byron preparing to rap on the door.

My curiosity nearly got the best of me. I waited a few days then deliberately slipped into my special gown. Like a spell of magic, there he stood at the door. At times I'd wear the same gown two nights in a row just to see what might happen. Each, and every time I wore that gown, he would appear. Sometimes I would wait for a week or more, but no matter what I did, I had the same result. He never surfaced when I wore my shorties, or any of my regular pajamas, or even another flannel. Like an old family recipe, I kept this secret to myself, and privately mused at the fact that I could somehow lure this wonderful boy to my threshold by simply repeating a wardrobe pattern.

Byron went away to college after high school, and I held onto that nightgown long after its hour to be tossed. It was a Velveteen Rabbit moment, I suppose.

Twice, I believe, after graduation, I dressed in that gown and sprawled across my bed to reminisce of days gone by, to recapture the feel and smell of youthful innocence… sensations that would not belong to me again. Twice, I believe, as I lay there alone with my thoughts, in my worn and faded gown, I heard a knock at the door. I held my breath and peered out the window to find Byron standing there… home for a break… to sit on the doorstep and visit once again.

3

MY FIRST MARRIAGE

It was basketball season in the fall of 1962. I was in the 8th grade. My friend Connie's older brother was a sophomore in high school and the star player on the varsity team. One evening I joined her for one of his games. One of her brother's friends noticed me sitting in the bleachers and asked him who I was. The next thing I knew that fella, who I had never met, called my mother to ask if he could come over to introduce himself. She welcomed him with open arms. He said the Beach Boys were going to be playing at a dance and asked her permission to take me. He was a sophomore… I would be turning 12 in December. Without asking how I felt about it, she said I could go but she would drive me there and pick me up when the dance was over.

My parents fell in love with him, and he became a permanent fixture for six years. After all, he was the son they never had. My mom was a beautiful and sexy woman, but she planted the seed of disgrace in my little bonnet about sex. Although there certainly was a goodly amount of making out, I remained a virgin through it all despite what anyone may have assumed.

When my boyfriend graduated in 1965, he joined the navy and was shipped off to Vietnam. I didn't know much about that war at the time, and I received only an occasional letter from him. I was 14 and I suppose it was an out-of-sight-out-of-mind experience. When he returned, he was stationed in Long Beach about two hours away. Shortly after I graduated in June of 1967, the wedding was planned for 150 of my parents' closest friends. The gala was to take place at the Airport Marina

Hotel in Marina del Rey. My gown had been purchased, and my bridal shower was superb. I was not included in any of the planning for my wedding, including guests I might like to have attend.

Shortly before the wedding, my fiancé disclosed to me that he had contracted a venereal disease when he was in Vietnam and assured me that he was fine. I was 17 years old and a virgin. I had saved myself for him… and he CHEATED on me… with a prostitute! My mother brushed it off like it was nothing. After all, he had been treated and all was good in the world. So, the wedding plans marched on, and I suffered in silence having no one to talk to… no one to listen, and no one to care.

Two weeks before the wedding for the invisible bride, Byron dropped by on a break from school. I hadn't seen him in probably a year. We sat outside by the pool and talked for a short while and then he left. My mother was so outraged that I would be "seeing someone" when I was to be married in a matter of days! She cancelled the wedding, sent back all the gifts and my gown. She instructed me to drive to Long Beach and return my ring to my fiancé IMMEDIATELY! In hindsight, I should have thanked her for that, but instead it became the impetus for self-inflicted destruction for years to come.

At that time, I was working as a checker at Alpha Beta Market. One of my co-workers was a very cute Patrick Swayze bad boy type from *Dirty Dancing*. He invited me to a movie, and I accepted. When he came to pick me up, my mother answered the door then closed it on him and forbid me to go out with him. That was the straw that broke the camel's back. Not only did we go out, but I moved into his parents' home and then he and I got a little place of our own. She called me a slut one night on the phone. I can't imagine I could have been beaten down any more than I already was, so I decided to marry him. Certainly, that would show her… something!

In September of 1969, I was 19, living in Hollywood, married and pregnant. My husband was otherwise occupied with his new love interest.

In my despair, I went to spend a weekend of consolation with my cousin Jeri in Berkeley. When I returned home, much to my horrified shock, his girlfriend had moved her belongings into our house. Neither of them was there when I arrived, and I proceeded to have an all-out mental breakdown.

My father came to pick me up and took me home to Lancaster, where my mother, who was 19 years my senior, was about to give birth to her fourth child.

Without so much as a courtesy conversation, my parents promptly arranged for me to fly to Mexico City for an abortion, as it was illegal in the United States. Apparently, no one seemed to think it might be an issue that needed my opinion or approval. I was generally invisible, and this was no exception. Since my mother certainly was not able to travel, my father escorted me. That alone made it more uncomfortable than it already was.

We had been told to check into a certain hotel and that someone would come to the lobby to pick me up. We were also told that once I arrived at the clinic, I would be allowed to call my father at any time.

In the late evening, we received a call from the lobby telling me to come downstairs… alone… conveniently providing no identity of the driver. Waiting in the lobby was a linebacker sort of man who spoke no English. I left in the night with a stranger, in a foreign country, who my father had not been allowed to see. Two other men had been waiting in the car as we drove off to an unknown destination. I was terrified. Sometime later, they pulled over to make a call from a pay phone. A few blocks further down the road we approached our destination where an electric gate opened and behind the 10-foot fenced perimeter sat a large villa. I was escorted into an office where another man sat behind a desk. Apparently, he was the boss man. He asked me if I had the cash. I handed him an envelope and he counted what was inside. Fearing for my life, I told him I had changed my mind and wanted to go back to the hotel. He told me it was too late to change my mind. I asked to call my father, and I was told that outgoing calls were not allowed. I insisted that I did not want to go through with the abortion, and he signaled his two men to take me into another room where they put me on a procedural bed and shackled my wrists and ankles. I struggled and fought the little bit I could while they injected sodium pentothal into my arm. When I awoke, I was taken back to the hotel and dropped off. I don't think I spoke a word for days. In fact, I was well into my adulthood before I seized the notion that I had a voice and that I mattered.

My mother took me to our family doctor for an exam when I got home. He said that the abortion was so botched up that he was fairly certain I would never be able to conceive again. A few days later, my mother gave birth to my sister Valerie. I got to share a bedroom with her for a torturous year… until I was able to run away from home… let the sex, drugs and rock 'n roll begin!

THE MIDDLE

Think of the power that's in the universe — moving the earth, growing the trees. And that's the same power within you, if you'll only have courage — and the will to use it

Charlie Chaplin

4

AN AMERICAN BUDDHIST IN LOS ANGELES

One of my favorite contemporary films is *An American Werewolf in London*. I suppose the greatest contrast to that, being an American Buddhist in Los Angeles, would be that one starts out as an animal – helpless, at the mercy of circumstances, the cycles of the moon and then transforms into a Human Being (not necessarily at the full moon, although it has been known to happen that way).

I am an American Buddhist in Los Angeles, and my experience has been just as hairy, grueling, painful, exciting, and humorous as was that of the gorgeous creature in the film, whose unfortunate destiny it was to experience just the opposite.

Under the moon of Pisces (I don't remember if it was full), I was born a werewolf-like creature in Santa Monica to two very normal American parents — divorced, broke, miserable, and confused. How much more American can you get?

Imagine this if you will. A werewolf-like creature (reactionary fangs in tow) is born into this world. Wherever it roams, it leaves willful mayhem in its tracks, and over time becomes a master of dodging silver bullets. One day, while in search of its next prey, it discovers a formula that will cure the ills of monster-like tendencies. It is promised! It is guaranteed! It has been factory tested! The creature takes the medicine and promptly buries it in a crack in the wall. Can anyone relate to such foolhardiness? I can… from personal experience, no less. It's embarrassing, but I never said I was born intelligent, I only said I was born in Santa Monica.

At this juncture I must share an observation about the American Buddhists in

Los Angeles… they are fearless. This group of laymen and laywomen have the incredible ability to completely disregard the function of fangs, claws, and drooling. They appear to see only the Beauty in the Beast. What an extraordinary group! As a matter of fact, that was precisely what I didn't like about them the most. They terrified me! Certainly, they looked like ordinary creatures; although, they did all have smiling eyes and warm hearts… putrid. The pack I ran with simply ripped those things out long before affording an opportunity to examine them.

These fearless, bright-eyed, warm-hearted Human Beings never retreated until their goals were met; their common goal being to mingle among the packs, diligently melting hearts of ice with the tools of their trade. They would risk the very possibility of having their own hearts torn out in their pursuit. It is a very difficult concept to understand. Most of us didn't have the time to try, as pouncing on prey was of so much more value. We must survive, right?

One of these American Buddhists in Los Angeles, armed with every trick in her book, challenged me head on. She told me her beautiful song possessed the power to end the pain and suffering of my nights, and that my torturous existence would, by contrast, become filled with a joy I would not otherwise know. I would need only to learn her melody and sing it each day with all my heart. She said her song held the secret to any dream coming true, any problem being overcome. I scoffed at this absurdity and made certain she had full view and was aware of the power in my fangs. I would have them all as my prey. My cunning wit was excited at the mere thought of winning this battle. I accepted her challenge.

As I carefully analyzed my strategy and cleverly prepared my plan of action, I knew this test would have to be presented with an impossibility. If my impossible goal was met, I would devote my life to their pledge. But, if my impossible goal was not met, they would all have to run with my pack.

Despite myself, and to my utter amazement, my impossible dream manifested completely. And much to my resistance, I began experiencing an unplanned emergence of a warm heart from the depths of my being. It was excruciating! I could feel the terror and pain of my life-long fangs receding, my claws becoming smooth, and my howling soothed to a gentle tone. I found myself attacking the suffering of others. I began piercing hearts with compassion instead of my fangs. I gave birth to a child with no fangs and no claws, although there was drooling. I found myself offering my home, my time, and my own heart to the encouragement of as many Human Beings and Potential Human Beings as I possibly could. This melody was habit forming, yet I have never seen even a single message from the Surgeon General to warn of its harm. I can't seem to shake it. I return to the pack nearly every day. I go armed with the same tool my friend once came to me with, as I fearlessly present the same challenge to others. Some cower, and with tail between their legs scurry off to hide in some dark cave. Some of them take me on.

I feel a full moon tonight… good… it has been a difficult month in search of that cave… now I will be able to light my way. Funny how things look so different to me now.

5

MY FIRST BUDDHIST MEETING

By the time I reached the ripe old age of 21, I had separated from my second husband. He was a pretty good guy. We got married when I was 20… he was 19. One of my high school friends was attending Sacramento State College and to escape my world of hell, I packed my bags, left town, and moved in with her and her boyfriend. Early one morning, there was a knock at my door. When I opened it, Richard stood on the stoop donning an impish grin. He was one the neighborhood guys I'd play basketball with next door in Lancaster. He convinced me that he was in love and in a grand attempt to squeeze my foot into the tiny glass slipper, we were married. I suppose the biggest problem for us was that we were far too young, and again my subconscious intention was to hurt my mother. But of course, when he didn't have the power to perform the magic trick of ensuring my happiness… naturally our relationship crumbled. I had also estranged myself from my family, and simply hated being alive.

Shortly after that time in 1974, my cousin Diane invited me to a Buddhist meeting. Although I had no idea what to expect, I thought it sounded just weird enough to be cool. The evening of the meeting, she picked me up and dropped me off at her apartment in Hollywood. She had neglected to tell me that she had someone else to pick up, so I was being pawned off on her friend Melvin, who would take me to the meeting.

Around 7:00 p.m., Melvin and I arrived at someone's home on Cadillac Street in West Los Angeles. Approaching the front door, I could hear a strange humming sound coming from inside the house. A sea of shoes covered the front porch. Following Melvin's lead, I stepped out of my shoes and trailed behind him to enter. What sounded like humming from the outside became a rather commanding mantra once we were inside.

The room was sardine-packed with people sitting on their knees, hands in prayer position, facing what looked like an altar encasing some sort of scroll. My cousin was already there and directed me to a small open spot on the floor next to her. She handed me a piece of paper which read Nam-myoho-renge-kyo. The people in the room chanted these words at a galloping clip. Diane pointed to the words on the paper in the rhythm and pace they were being chanted so that I could follow along. Was she kidding? There was no way I could discern that what she was pointing to could be the same booming sound I was hearing. The power of the vibration in the room was undeniable.

After a few minutes of that chant, a bell rang, and everyone began to recite strange words from a little book. My mind spun as my cousin continued pointing to the blur of letters passing on the page as if I were standing roadside watching race cars zooming by. Exactly what had she fallen into?

The chanting soon ended, and a lively procession of people began popping up… some explaining the whys and wherefores of our being there, some shared experiences of finding great jobs, better living situations, overcoming illnesses, but most importantly a deep sense of happiness that came from their chanting those peculiar words to the scroll in the altar. Listening to multitudes of joyous experiences made me want to puke. By contrast, my darkness and despair stood out like a sore thumb. There was nothing I wanted more than to make a beeline and dash out the escape hatch.

All it took for me to do just that was for one young woman, Bille Jo, to approach me at the close of the meeting and ask how I enjoyed it. Enjoy it?! My eyes welled up and I darted out of the house as fast as I could run.

Diane tried many times over the next year to encourage me to attend another gathering, but I simply could not. Why would she take me to such a place to make a mockery of my misery? Why would she do something like that? How cruel!

6

THE HAWAII
CONVENTION

Over the course of the following year, my life condition had sunk to an all-time low. Everything was wrong! Everything was displaced!

I had been working for an absolutely insane doctor out in Encino for about a year. I hated getting up in the morning. He was a speaking-in-tongues Evangelical who looked like Charles Manson. One morning at the office with a room filled with annoyed patients, he casually strolled in three hours late. All aglow he announced that while he was on his hospital rounds, the elevator doors opened without his having to push the button. He was convinced he was the Second Coming of Christ. I grabbed my purse and headed for the hills.

I had a great little place just a few blocks from Santa Monica Beach that I was going to have to forsake. As I neared my quarter century birthday, I was about to be divorced for the second time. I didn't have two nickels to rub together, and I could not have been any more miserable.

Reluctantly I called my cousin Diane and asked if she would meet me for lunch. Having not spoken in nearly a year (at my request), and despite my bad behavior, much to my surprise she agreed to meet me.

We sat at a restaurant on the patio. She didn't seem to have much to say, so I occupied the air space and upchucked my hopelessness. As the end of her lunch hour approached, she announced that she needed to leave. And then, almost in passing, she mentioned that she was going to Hawaii for a few days to a Buddhist convention. She was clearly on Cloud Nine. I sat there wondering what my Bohemian, musician cousin could possibly find so enticing about a stuffy ballroom filled with sweaty old men in tuxedos, carting cigars, and martinis, while groping at the asses of young women. Isn't that a convention? What had they done to my cousin? They must have sucked her brains out.

A few weeks after her return, she called to let me know the Buddhist group was going to be showing a film of the Hawaii Convention at the Santa Monica Civic Auditorium. She asked if I would be her date. I agreed to go, if for no other reason than to see the goings on in that hotel ballroom. Little did I know that my life was about to become forever changed.

The Santa Monica Civic Auditorium seats 3,000 people, and let me tell you, it was standing room only. As the Big Screen came to life, a microcosm of a world in peace sprawled across it. Somehow, these Buddhists had convinced the Hawaiian government to allow them to build a floating island twice the size of a football field in pristine Waikiki Bay. Their purpose was to stage a pageant of American history through song and dance in honor of America's Bicentennial that would fall on the Fourth of July the following year — 1976.

Having been a product of the Vietnam War, Flower Power and all the disenchantment that went with it, I found myself deeply overwhelmed by what I saw. The music and dance were so beautifully orchestrated. The costumes and stage settings were incredible. And I learned the performers mostly were ordinary people trained in only their art of elevating the spirit of humanity. Each, and every person on that stage poured their hearts and souls into their performances. It was spectacular! What made this "convention" especially stunning was not only the exquisite performances, but the vision of the 100,000 spectators blanketing the beach — a complete cross-section of humanity — every color and hue, religion, language, male, female, young and old — arm in arm, joyfully weeping at the possibility of such a world. I desperately wanted some of that!

7

MY SECOND
BUDDHIST MEETING

From the time I was in high school, I had always been hired on the spot for every job I ever applied for. I was a back office medical assistant at that time, and I could not find a job. A smattering of reasons thrown out at me were: "You're too tall," "You're too short," "You're not a blonde," "You're too fat," "You're too skinny," "This is a podiatry office and you've only worked for family practice." ALL RIGHT ALREADY! (A little hyperbole never hurt anything.)

Shortly before I went to the Santa Monica Civic with my cousin, on recommendation from a friend, I made an appointment with a psychologist. I had never been in counseling before and wasn't sure what to expect, but my guess was that I would spew my awful life all over her comfy couch. As it turned out, she specialized in primal scream therapy… the stark opposite of what I would come to learn about Buddhism. Primal scream is a method of drawing out the darkest part of your psyche theoretically releasing it through tremendous force and violence. It took the therapist a lot of coaxing to get me to unleash the rage that had been festering for years. She certainly succeeded in opening Pandora's Box. The venom that gushed out of me was terrifying and I was mortified by what I thought I might be capable of. That kind of treatment should be criminalized in any society!

With the remnants of that episode looming, I sucked up what might be left of me and, with tail between my legs, found my way to a second Buddhist meeting.

When the supersonic chanting came to an end, one of the Buddhists said there is no such thing as an impossible dream with the practice of chanting Nam-myoho-renge-kyo!

I learned that Nam-myoho-renge-kyo is a natural law of the universe… like E=MC2. It's the law of cause and effect. You know, for every action there is an equal and opposite reaction. That pretty much describes karma. So, everything that happens in our lives… good, bad, or indifferent… we need to pat ourselves on the back and take credit for it. It's not about guilt or shame… or boasting… it's merely acknowledging that it belongs to us. The good news is, if we created it, we can un-create it, we can enhance it, or we can create something new.

The phrase Nam-myoho-renge-kyo is the essence of the Lotus Sutra, which is the final and most important teaching of the round, happy Buddha we're all familiar with. It is the name of our inherent enlightened life condition. When we chant that phrase, it's like an alarm clock that jars us from a deep sleep, it arouses our energy, compassion, and wisdom… and it happens despite ourselves. Like any respectable natural law, understanding the intricacies of it are not a requirement. For instance, electricity and gravity have always existed, but we humans have not always enjoyed the benefits of them until someone figured out how to harness it. Even having harnessed them, we common mortals still don't need to know anything more than flipping a switch magically produces light or jumping off a roof pulls you in only one direction.

Wow! That was a lot to take in!

I was dared to give it a try for three months… as prescribed… and if I did not experience tremendous results in that time, the leader of the meeting said he would stop practicing with me. I took the challenge and received my own scroll called a Gohonzon on August 30, 1975.

When I decided to take the test drive with this Buddhist practice, I committed to myself that I would follow the recipe to the letter. I was not going to be the one whose just desserts were not sweet because I elected to omit a crucial ingredient. In my spiteful skepticism, I would prove it didn't work BECAUSE I did it right! From the get-go, I chanted an abundance of Nam-myoho-renge-kyo. I learned the little book and smugly found myself filled with pride when I set into memory a portion of the sutra. I was energized when I chanted and even more so when I chanted with a group.

That didn't change the fact that I still did not have a job and I still had to move from my apartment.

8

THE PARKING METER

My cousin Jeri was married to John, a doctor doing his residency at Kaiser Permanente on Sunset Boulevard.

A few days after beginning to prove the absurdity of chanting strange words to a piece of paper, John suggested I file a job application with Kaiser.

After wallowing in my pity party for a minute, I borrowed a few dollars from a neighbor to feed my VW Bug so I could make it from Santa Monica to Sunset Boulevard and Vermont.

Kaiser is a humongous medical facility taking up a few city-blocks worth of buildings. Finding parking in Los Angeles was generally impossible. All street parking is metered, and garage parking is unaffordable unless you own the building. The only other alternative I could see would have been to walk from just about where I started — in Santa Monica. I circled around the block a few times, to no avail, before deciding it might be a good time to test those words… Nam-myoho-renge-kyo, Nam-myoho-renge-kyo. As the clock was about to strike noon, I made another circle around the facility, and there, right at the front door, a car pulled away from the curb. Putting the pedal to the medal, I snatched it. I got out of the car chanting under my breath hoping I could sneak in, complete an application, and be out the door before a meter maid came around in search of filling her quota. Then I saw it. The meter had an hour of time left… my first benefit!

Wandering aimlessly through the maze of corridors, I finally found my way to Human Resources. A woman welcomed me to complete an application, but she said there were no openings. She did offer to say that if anything came up, they would call me. *Yeah, I'm sure you will!* As I turned in the application, she appeared to have had an afterthought. She promptly sent me to see the supervisor in the Surgical Walk-In Clinic, which is a step down from emergency care.

When I arrived at my destination, Mrs. King, the supervisor, said she had no idea why I had been sent there as she had no openings. *Of course, you don't!* As I stood to leave, she appeared to have an afterthought. She offered that she could put me on as an "on-call" receptionist, meaning that should anyone call in sick, go on vacation, maternity leave, drop dead… I could fill in. In sheer desperation, I said, "I'll take it!" She did make it perfectly clear that there would be no way to know when, or even if, I would ever be called. I thanked her, said I understood, and dashed out the door. When I realized how long I had been in there, I began mumbling Nam-myoho-renge-kyo under my breath hoping my windshield had not been garnished with a little pink ticket. Lo and behold, one hour still remained on the meter. The darned thing was stuck, and I was in some kind of newfound rhythm.

9

LITERAL TRANSLATION NO. 1

Pulling away from the broken meter, I drove down the street a couple of blocks where I pulled into a driveway to maneuver a turn around when I noticed a For Rent sign on the front lawn of a charming Spanish duplex. Amazing! Walking distance from the job I just got that I may never be called for. How cool is that? I parked my car and went up to the door of the lower unit.

A friendly sort of guy gave me a tour of the upper unit. It was a spacious two-bedroom apartment. Being the honest girl that I am, I explained my situation: I had a kinda sorta job at Kaiser that I may or may not be called for, I had to move from my apartment, I would certainly need a roommate to be able to afford this great place just two blocks from my kinda sorta job. For some bizarre, unknown reason he removed the sign, said he had a good feeling about me, and said I could move in over the weekend. Shaking my head in disbelief, I said, "Sure, why not? We can work it out."

At that point it was getting to be late in the day. Traffic to my Buddhist meeting was going to be brutal, and I didn't want to be late. I chanted Nam-myoho-renge-kyo all the way. My focus was to be hired at Kaiser full time and figure out some way to move into that duplex. Even if I had a job, I couldn't afford that rent without a roommate.

I removed my shoes at the door, and scurried in. Diane was already there and had saved an if-you-can-squeeze-into-this-space-on-the-floor-it's-yours spot. I managed to squeeze in right behind Ben Frank, who was leading the meeting. When we finished chanting, he turned around to face the room. Ben was a character actor and generally remained true to character even in his off-camera life… rugged good looks, gravelly voice… a tough guy persona.

Ben began to explain how chanting Nam-myoho-renge-kyo works. He described it like this: "If I'm window shopping and I see you across the street… let's say your name is Robert… and I'm desperately trying to get your attention by calling out, 'SAMMY! SAMMY!' there's a good chance you won't turn around… that's not your name… why would you respond to it? So, it's the same premise… by calling out the correct name of your own highest potential, your enlightened life, even if you don't believe it, it wakes up and responds in kind… just like gravity, it works 100% of the time whether you believe it or not. The proof is in the pudding, as it were."

I know that if my intention is to do my best to impress someone, I'm going to spend some time putting on just the right amount of makeup and having my hair look great, then pick something to wear that will be the most flattering on my bod. Believe me when I say that to successfully accomplish that, I MUST have a good mirror or disaster will ensue. With that in mind, we MUST have a good mirror to clearly see the inside of us.

In 13th century Japan, a Buddhist monk named Nichiren Daishonin realized that once a great teacher passes, we ordinary humans generally erect statutes and symbols to worship in their stead… oftentimes resulting in the individual relinquishing their own responsibility to awaken the boundless power and greatness within to the statuary to bestow blessings. Nichiren created a mirror of the human condition in the form of a scroll for practitioners to focus on. Chanting to it is like taking a bottle of Windex to a schmutz-caked mirror to better see just how our eyebrows and lipstick are turning out.

I also learned that to test any philosophy or practice, there are three essential truths: there must be theoretical proof that completely pans out in everyday reality, and that it is thoroughly documented by the teacher, otherwise what we get is a long line of playing "telephone." But the most important proof is actual proof. In other words, when the documented theory is applied, what happens? Nichiren's humanistic teachings absolutely guarantee that every human has boundless potential and that if the recipe to that means is followed correctly, every area of our lives will overflow with tremendous benefit. And when you watch your own life blossom beyond your wildest dreams, you naturally want to share that with other people so they too will experience profound benefit.

Ben looked at me and asked how long I had been chanting. I sheepishly replied, "Technically, only a few minutes." He asked my age, and I told him I was 25. His eyes were penetrating. Then he mused, "Imagine you have been living in a place all your life… you've never had electricity and there are no windows… so, the house has always been as dark as a cave… but like someone having no sight, you would have long ago found your way around… you would have no problem functioning in the dark. Then one day someone tells you about a little switch on the wall (Nam-myo-ho-renge-kyo). *Drum roll* For the first time, the lights are switched on. After an entire lifetime of living in the dark, what exactly do you think you might see? My guess would be indescribable filth… cockroaches crawling everywhere. It's always been there… you just never knew it. So now you have a choice… you always have a choice. Either you roll up your sleeves and get started with the cleanup, or you flip the switch off and pretend you never saw it. Just because you turn the switch doesn't mean the filth and roaches disappear. Now, what would you like to do?" I swallowed hard as I attempted to digest his vivid analogy of what happens when one begins to chant Nam-myoho-renge-kyo.

Just then a young woman jumped up to share her experience. She was a college student making fantastic grades and she had a job. She lived at home, but she really wanted to venture out on her own. She was looking for a roommate. *Ta Da!!!* I accosted her right after the meeting.

The following day I took her to see the apartment and we arranged to move in over the weekend.

Bright and early the next morning, my phone rang with a call from Mrs. King at Kaiser. One of her receptionists was pregnant and had been ordered to bed rest for the duration of her pregnancy. She needed me to come in and work that day. That day lasted for about five years.

Early Saturday morning, my new roommate and I hauled our belongings into our new abode. We dropped everything and headed out to our Buddhist activities. Returning home that evening, we flipped on the lights. Can you guess? Cockroaches were hustling and bustling EVERYWHERE! Let me tell you, I would take on a tiger before I'd take on crawling things. Despite what Ben Frank had said, without hesitation, I switched the lights off and ran to my mothers in Santa Monica as fast as my little 8 ½'s could carry me.

10

THE MAN
IN THE
UROLOGY
DEPARTMENT

As I explained before, in my quest to prove these Buddhists senseless, I demanded every morning as I chanted that something extraordinary would happen on that day. So far, so good… although, I refused to equate chanting to a piece of paper as having anything to do with it.

After a half day of training for my new on-call position, they released me into the wild to fend for myself. I greeted patients, determined the priority of their emergency, and checked them in accordingly.

Shortly after I arrived on my second day, Mrs. King said that the receptionist in the Urology Department had called in sick. She asked me to please go to that department and fill in until that on-call person arrived, and then return to my post. I wandered through the halls until I found the Urology Department. Just as I got there, a patient who had seen a doctor asked me to help him fill out some forms for an upcoming surgery. I was happy to assist.

One of the questions on the form asked where the patient was born. He responded, "Greece." Without looking up, I matter-of-factly told him that I was half Greek. To his delight, he asked my last name. Explaining that my biological parents were divorced when I was a baby, I said, "Tasulis." His delight moved up a notch to enthusiasm as he went on to say his best friend was Chris Tasulis. Still not looking up from the form, I told him my father's name was George and I doubted they

37

were related. Just then, the on-call person came in and I returned to the Surgical Walk-In clinic. I was only there long enough to meet that man.

Around three o'clock in the afternoon, I received a phone call from him. He said he had been looking for me all day, but no one knew who I was. Maybe because I wasn't a "real" employee? Anyway, he said he had just talked to my grandmother… Chris was my father's brother! That was a fairly interesting response to my morning demand of the universe. I thanked him for calling, but I had no interest in meeting any of those people. I did call my mom after work to tell her about my crazy day. She thought it was pretty crazy, too.

Side bar: A few months before, my mom and six-year-old sister, Valerie, had moved from Lancaster to Santa Monica. My parents had split up. My mom was a manicurist and had been working next door to a small café. Every morning after dropping Valerie off at school, she would sit at the counter and chit-chat with the owner while she had a bagel and coffee before going to work.

A few days after I met the Greek, Valerie had a dental appointment in Westchester. Since they were new to the area, it was her first visit. Meandering through the hallways of the medical building looking for the right suite, my mom noticed the sign on one of the doors that read, Chris Tasulis, Optometrist. Curiously, they went in to find her former brother-in-law and his wife, Helen. After telling them my story of a few days before, they joyfully said they knew all about it from their friend. As the conversation progressed, it was discovered that the Kaiser patient I met was the owner of the little café in Santa Monica and happened to be the person my mom sat and chit-chatted with every morning.

Considering the fact that I worked near downtown Los Angeles, my mom lived in Santa Monica, and my uncle's office was in Westchester, yes, it was astounding, and certainly a bit over-the-top, but nonetheless, I had no interest in meeting any of them. Proof of something? Perhaps. But in my opinion, it had nothing to do with chanting.

11
LITERAL TRANSLATION NO. 2

After the cockroach debacle, I was fortunate enough to impose upon my mom in Santa Monica until I could find another place.

My cousin Jeri and her Kaiser doctor hubby, John, lived in a charming old-world Spanish duplex in Echo Park up in the hills of downtown Los Angeles. Echo Park is one of the oldest and eclectic neighborhoods in the L.A. area. Its rolling hills are swathed with Victorian, turn-of-the-century, and revival era architecture. It unquestionably inspires an imaginary passage into another time. In fact, the Michael Jackson Thriller House is just around the corner from where Jeri and John lived. Their lot accommodated three structures: an upper and lower Spanish duplex at the street level, a side-by-side Spanish duplex situated on the far rear of the property (which they occupied), and in between a small wood-framed cottage—I'd imagine a caretaker residence in the early 1900s.

A few days after moving in with my mom, Jeri called with a possible lead for a rental. The cute little wood-framed cottage in front of them was empty. She explained that most of Echo Park had been purchased by the Department of Transportation because at some point, they planned to tear down all that amazing history and fill it up with more freeways. Until then, the city was renting the properties out cheap with the tenants' understanding, of course, that they could be forced to leave at any time. She said there was a long wait list to get in, but it might be worth my while to check it out.

I promptly contacted the Department to complete an application, mentioning my particular interest in the little wood-framed house.

Within a couple of days, the Department of Transportation contacted me to say that a glowing reference from Jeri and John, whose track record was impeccable, had pushed my application through and that little gem was mine! The rent was $80 a month. Even for those days, that was a basement bargain price and I moved right in.

On the Friday evening after I moved in, I attended another meeting with Ben Frank as the leader. Again, I squeezed myself right in front of the room. When the chanting ended, Ben singled me out, again.

On this occasion, he chose a new and improved analogy. It went something like this:

Ben: "Imagine your life is a hose… a hose that has been lying at the bottom of a swamp… how old did you say you were?"

Me: "Twenty-five."

Ben: "Ok, for twenty-five years you, the hose, have been sitting at the bottom of this swamp. What would you imagine the hose might be filled with? Most likely it would be putrid muck, wouldn't you say? You don't necessarily notice the muck as it simply has always been there for you to wallow in. Then one day someone finds this hose and hooks it up to a water faucet and turns it on full blast. What do you suppose might happen? Yes, the muck begins to shoot out the other end. But what do you think is pushing it out? Fresh, clean water."

I suppose his analogy made sense. I digested his words and went home.

The next morning was Saturday. There were all day activities going on with my Buddhist group and as I prepared to leave my cute little house for the day, I heard what sounded like a small explosion coming from the bathroom.

I went to see what had happened… and there before my eyes was raw sewage spewing over the sides of my bathtub! Aaaaaaaahhhhhhh! I thought I was going to puke and pass out all at the same time. Naturally, the fact that my new landlord was a bureaucracy, no one would be available to assist in this disaster until Monday morning.

Before puking and passing out, I frantically found a plumber from the Yellow Pages, and someone came to my rescue in what seemed a matter of minutes. He was able to fix the problem in fairly short order. But he made it clear he didn't clean up that kind of shit. He didn't actually call it that… but hey, let's call it like it is. So, I tied a scarf around my nose and mouth, put on some heavy-duty gloves and spent hours sterilizing my cute little bathroom. Finishing up with my last swipe and bottle of bleach, I properly disposed of all the nasty rags.

Still determined to make it to the Buddhist activity even if I was going to be late, I opened my front door to leave but heard a small explosion. NOOOOOooooooooo! With an ache in my heart and a knot in my stomach, I summoned every ounce of courage I could muster. I dragged myself back into the bathroom. Much to my disbelief, a spray of clean, fresh water spewed from the pipe behind the toilet.

After telephonically walking me through the process of shutting off the water valve, the plumber headed back over for the second fix of the day.

FINALLY, I headed out the door, chanting all the way to the meeting in hopes that Ben Frank would not be leading our meeting that night.

12

THE PAP SMEAR

It's important to be an active participant and advocate for our own health, and it should be coupled with the best medical professionals we can surround ourselves with. However, if our lives lack good fortune, even with the best of the best onboard, we might be the ones who slip through the cracks and find ourselves unnecessarily at the mercy of a fine doctor having his own personal terrible day.

Not long after I began working at Kaiser, I made an appointment for a long overdue physical exam. It was 1975 B.C. (before children), and I was 25.

My routine pap smear revealed dysplasia or precancerous lesions. My doctor said we needed to repeat the test just to be sure. So, we did, and the second test came back the same.

The next step in the process was to have cryosurgery, which freezes off the bad cells, and once they fall away, typically the new healthy cells should be just fine. Well, they weren't.

Step three was a cervical biopsy to identify exactly what was going on. The biopsy revealed the same result, and the suggested treatment was to have a complete hysterectomy to avoid the worst possible scenario.

Terrified of what my fate might be, especially at such a young age, I upped the amount of time I spent chanting Nam-myoho-renge-kyo adding a fierce determination to turn poison into medicine.

I agreed to the surgery and a pre-op was scheduled a couple of days before that date. When I arrived for my pre-op, I found out that the doctor I had been seeing had left Kaiser and I now had a new replacement doctor.

After talking with him for quite some time, he suggested he do one more pap smear just for good luck. During my exam, he spotted a little discharge that he wanted to look at under the microscope. When he came back, he said I had a minor bacterial infection and told me we needed to clear it up before going into a sterile surgical environment. The medication was for a 10-day period, and I was scheduled for a return pre-op at that time. Upon my return, the doc wanted to run another pap smear… it came back perfectly normal. The insignificant bacterial infection had been throwing off the results of all the previous tests. There was NOTHING wrong with me. The other doctor was ready, willing, and able to remove all my working parts for absolutely no good reason, except that it would have been my misfortune. My fortune was reflected in the changing of the guard at the crucial moment.

13

THE SUNSHINE
OF MY LIFE

My sister, Nancy, was brain-damaged in a car accident when she was 18 months old, leaving her blind and mentally challenged. For several years she lived at the Foundation for the Junior Blind. Ordinarily, the residents were phased out at the age of 18, but Nancy had an irresistible way about her, and I'm sure because of that, they let her slide under the radar and allowed her to stay until she was 21. That was in March 1976.

Oddly, as the time drew near for Nancy's phase-out, my parents had only just discovered there were no facilities in existence for multi-handicapped blind adults. Not sure why they waited so long to explore their options. Anyway, what they learned about their choices was… "there weren't any!" There were state institutions, (that was never going to happen); board and care homes (Nancy was not self-sufficient enough to live in that capacity); or live at home (both of my parents worked, and again, Nancy could not be left alone). Nothing doable there.

As I continued my daily toe dunking to test the waters of my Buddhist practice, I decided this was just the proof-is-in-the-pudding result I needed to convince myself this Buddhism had any merit.

Bill Young, the Director of the Foundation for the Junior Blind, called a meeting for the families of the residents to present a proposal he had been working on for the first adult facility of its kind in the country. Impeccable timing! I didn't see the connection, but just as I was told it would happen, as soon as I began to put forth more effort into my practice, my first obstacle arose. My mother!

∧ ∧ ∧

A little more than a month after being hired as an on-call receptionist at Kaiser, I applied for a permanent position as a billing clerk in the Kaiser Insurance Department. My supervisor, Bob, was an arrogant not-very-nice smug kind of guy. Somehow, I survived him for more than four years.

My mom called me at work one day. She had an uncanny way about certain things… button pushing things that made me want to stay away. Both of my parents were less than enthused about my Buddhist practice and neither of them were shy about it. After all, according to my dad, "The Japanese bombed Pearl Harbor." According to my not-religious-culturally-Jewish mother, "You are Jewish, you know?"

The Insurance Billing Department was a long narrow room with desks lining either side of a middle walkway that led to an office with a large picture window where King Bob sat facing his subjects.

Back to the call…

"This is Debbie. May I help you?"

"It's your mother!"

I could tell instinctively that this was going to be one of those button pushing moments. Why couldn't she wait until I got home? Nope, it's way more effective to upset someone while they're at work.

"I wanted to tell you that Bill Young is calling a meeting to present a proposal for the first facility in the country for multi-handicapped blind adults. You might want to think about getting involved and do something worthwhile in your life and forget about this chanting nonsense."

I'm not sure I even responded. Most likely I just hung up. Mission accomplished! I couldn't concentrate on anything except jumping up and down and screaming at the top of my lungs. After all, I was born a volcanic reactionary. And I was quite good at it. She always had an emotional stranglehold on me, even if I was a quarter of a century old. Asthma generally followed an explosion of my pent-up-ed-ness.

There is no reasonable explanation for the bizarre and curious events that followed… except for one… I was chanting Nam-myoho-renge-kyo.

^ ^ ^

Donning my I'll-show-you attitude, I picked up the phone and called Motown Records in Hollywood. I have no idea where that came from. The switchboard operator answered, and I wasn't sure what to do next. When all else fails, wing it!

> "Hi. I'd like to speak with whoever is in charge of Stevie Wonder doing a benefit concert."

> "Please hold the line while I put you through to his business manager."

> *WHAT! Are you kidding me? Now what?!*

> "Hi. This is Reggie."

> *Think… THINK…*

> "Hi, my name is Debbie Torres. I am… *(who am I?)*… the assistant to Bill Young… the Director of the Foundation for the Junior Blind. We are in the process of establishing the first facility for multi-handicapped blind adults in the country. We're interested in discussing the possibility of Stevie doing a benefit concert for us."

That 30-second silence felt like at least 10 minutes.

> "Hmmmm. That might be something he could get behind. Why don't you come in tomorrow afternoon at about 3:00 so we can talk about it?"

> "Uh, sure, that would be… great!"

ARE YOU KIDDING ME!!!

"Yes, we'll be there. Thank you… thank you! THANK YOU!"

Jumping up and down and screaming remained on the table as extremes were generally my go-to. I glanced through the window at the king as he glared back in his normal contemptible fashion. The good news about my job was that I spent most of my time on the phone. Diverting eye contact, I chanted under my breath as I called Bill Young.

"Hi, it's Debbie Torres. What are you doing tomorrow around 3:00?"

"My calendar is clear. Why?"

"We have a meeting with Stevie Wonder's business manager to discuss him doing a benefit concert!"

The vulture king looked up from his perch behind the window. He must have heard the thud Bill Young made as he fell off his chair. As we both sat there on the floor, I had to think of a way to leave work early so I could meet him at Motown. That part was a piece of cake.

∧ ∧ ∧

At 3:00 the next day, Bill and I were warmly greeted at Motown by Reggie and Chris. Both were quite interested in learning more about the potential of this prototype facility. What they needed from us was an audiotape explaining our story and our vision for Stevie's participation. All presentations were made to him in that manner. Made sense to me.

That night I upped the stakes of my impossible dream! I made a card to place on my chanting altar with the names: Stevie Wonder, Sammy Davis Jr., and Herbie Hancock. Why them? Why not? Stevie was blind, Sammy Davis was blind in one eye, and Herbie Hancock… well, he was my new favorite jazz artist. On a second card to put on my altar, I wrote: PROFOUND, UNFATHOMABLE, UNPREC-EDENTED, IMMEASURABLE, EXTRAORDINARY VICTORY!

∧ ∧ ∧

After the tremendous success of the pre-Bicentennial pageant in Hawaii, the Buddhist organization I belong to was invited to sponsor the Bicentennial Celebration for New York City over the Fourth of July weekend in 1976. Warehouses were buzzing all over Los Angeles and New York City. Members were creating and constructing magnificent floats and set designs, painting building-sized backdrops, and stitching costumes for thousands of performers reflecting the colorful and diverse cultures of America. Dance teams, choruses, brass bands, and orchestras were rehearsing nationwide. People of all ages, races, nationalities, and backgrounds worked passionately to bring about a celebration equal to none.

I spent every waking moment after work and on weekends painting props, running electrical wires through billboard-sized murals, hand-stitching sequins on hats and sewing miniature light bulbs in costumes.

∧ ∧ ∧

One afternoon a group of us, who had been diligently working at one of the warehouses, took a break to grab a bite to eat. I didn't know any of them. The customary course of conversation at any Buddhist gathering resorted to: "So, what benefits have you gotten since you started chanting?"

When all eyes fell on me, I blurted out my I'll-show-you-mom tale… up to that point, of course. One of the guys sitting across from me was Holden. I found out he was the conga player for Papa John Creech and the Midnight Sun. After listening to my story, he said, "Ray Maldonado is a good friend of mine. He's Stevie's band director." He wrote something on a piece of paper and handed it to me. "Here's his phone number. Just tell him I told you to call." *Seriously? Okay!* I tucked his number away for safe keeping and continued to devour my sandwich… pinching myself between each bite.

A couple of nights later, I was painting palm leaves for one of the sets. Herman, a fellow painter, asked about my benefits. Once again, well, you know the drill. Lo and behold, Herman casually mentioned, "Stevie's bodyguard is one of my best friends. I know he'll do whatever he can to help you."

Wow! Just WOW! Not sure how that might manifest, but I was elated to exchange phone numbers.

^ ^ ^

In the meantime, Bill made the audiotape addressed to Stevie. Then I found out from Herman that Stevie was wrapping up the recording of his new album and would be leaving town the next night. Somehow, I had to get the tape to him before he left. The plan was that the bodyguard would pick up the tape from me at work the next day and personally put it in Stevie's hands. But about 4:30 the next afternoon, Herman called to tell me that his friend's car broke down in Rancho Cucamonga. There was no possible way he would get back before Stevie's departure. *DAMN! Now what do I do?! Hmmm… chant?*

^ ^ ^

Dave Blumberg was one of my Buddhist leaders. He was also a notable music arranger. I was sure he would know where Stevie recorded. After chanting all the way home from work, I drummed up the nerve to call him. Naturally, he had no intention of giving me that information. But, after I flailed around on the floor kicking and begging, he said, "Okay, I'll give you the names of three studios. If you find him, great, and you do know, I did not tell you anything!"

Let the scavenger hunt begin. I opened the phone book (for those of you less than 30-ish, it was a directory of phone numbers and addresses of individuals and businesses in your community) to look up the numbers of the studios. I scored on the first call. A woman named Josette answered the phone. I explained that Chris and Reggie had asked me to deliver a tape to Stevie and I wanted to know if he might be there. She told me he was and invited me to drop it off any time before 9:00 p.m. Holy schamoly Batman! I chanted for an hour and then headed out to the studio.

Josette was at the front desk when I arrived. I introduced myself, and as I handed her the tape, she asked me if I'd like to go in. *Go in? What does that mean?* Sure! Why not? Escorting me into the observation side of the recording studio, I saw and heard Stevie Wonder recording what was soon to be released… *Songs in the Key of Life.* I was the only one in the room. Pinching myself was becoming a habit I could sorely get used to.

A while later, a musician came in and sat down next to me. He asked if I was a singer. I said, "No?" He asked if I was related to someone at the studio. I said, "No?" Then he asked why I was there, and the empty bubble hovering over my head filled with text, as I read aloud, "Do you know Ray Maldonado?"

He said Ray was standing right outside the door and asked if I wanted to talk to him. Of course, I do! We left the room, and Ray and I were properly introduced. I told him I was a friend of Holden's. Apparently, that was all I needed to say. Whatever he could do… he was at my disposal. I told him about the tape, and he asked me to walk down the street with him so he could get some coffee. On the way out the door, he grabbed the tape. As we walked back to the studio, he suggested we get into his car and listen to it. When he finished listening, he sat for a moment and then said, "This is terrible! If you want to grab Stevie's attention, find someone who isn't afraid to speak into a mic. Trust me on this! You DO NOT want to give this to him!"

He handed the tape back to me and we went our separate ways. Although I was consumed with disappointment, I sensed the universe had my back and that I had been protected from a looming disaster.

So, there I was… Stevie was leaving town… I was leaving town with 30,000 of my closest friends… and we were all heading for the Big Apple.

∧ ∧ ∧

That night, I once again was graced with my recurring nightmare of a mob of monster-like people chasing me. They were on my heels, and I could not run any faster. I could barely breathe. I flapped my arms up and down as I had so many other times, and as I slowly rose beyond their reach, my weary arms struggled to keep myself from their grip, and as usual, the telephone wires were crisscrossed like mesh. I couldn't fly through it. It was too dangerous. I was exhausted and knew I could not go on. I reached behind me and pulled forth a giant pair of scissors. I clipped the wires and watched them fall away like ribbons, and for the first time, I flew up and away from the menacing crowd below.

I never had that dream again.

∧ ∧ ∧

We descended upon New York on July 2, 1976.

One of our many staged events was set up on Wall Street. I was an alto in the chorus. Behind the stage, we lined up waiting for our turn to go on when I heard an amazing jazz ensemble playing. We were up next. As that act left the stage for us to go on, Herbie Hancock passed by me. I had no idea he was one of us Buddhists. In disbelief, I touched his arm and whispered that I needed to talk to him. He quickly wrote his number on a small piece of paper and told me to call him in September when he returned from touring. Had I been sitting in a chair, surely, it would have toppled over… so pinching would simply have to do.

The next morning, before the activities of the day began, I was scurrying my way through the continental breakfast line along with hundreds of other Buddhists from all over the country. A woman sat down next to me, and we struck up a conversation. She asked me about, well, you know what. Repeating my story, I added the latest tidbit. She told me she was a manicurist in Beverly Hills. She also told me that Sammy Davis, Jr.'s business manager's wife had been her client for years. We traded phone numbers and she said she would call me when we got home. What a rush!

∧ ∧ ∧

It was the Fourth of July. America's 200-year anniversary. Our main event would be a first time ever nighttime parade down the Avenue of the Americas. Elizabeth Taylor, Gloria Swanson, Cab Calloway, Rick Monday, Roberta Flack, and several others, were our guests of honor riding in our magnificent parade. A million people lined the Avenue of the Americas to cheer us on as gorgeous floats and hundreds of dancers and marching bands sporting electrified costumes paraded their way through Manhattan. Never in my life had I been filled with such energy and passion. This movement for peace was just what the doctor ordered for my life to wake up and shake up and explode with extraordinary, bigger than life tales.

The next day, we flaunted a spectacular production between a double-header Yankee game at Shea Stadium. Hundreds of us danced and sang in a pageant of American history. This new momentum was mind boggling. My journey to realize impossible dreams was unfolding.

The first thing on my checklist when we got home was to call my Auntie Gogi. She was a popular singer in the 1950s, knocking Elvis off the charts in 1956 with her hit *The Wayward Wind*. Obviously, she had no fear of a mic… so, I asked if she would make the tape for Stevie. I was surprised when she said, "Stevie Wonder wouldn't know who I am. Let me see if Jeff Bridges will do it."

This was just getting better by the minute. When I was 16, one of my high school girlfriends and I stayed at my Auntie Gogi's house over spring break. The Bridges were neighbors of my aunt and had been dear friends for decades. Jeff and Beau came over to hang out with us in the pool. I was swimming under water from one end of the pool to the other when Jeff swam up to me and we kissed… a mermaid/merman moment of sorts. Had I known he was going to be Jeff Bridges when he grew up, I may have played my cards a bit differently. Anyway, Jeff was happy to make the tape. And he did.

Before I could check off the next item on my list, the manicurist called. Her client was all too happy to give me her husband's number. After spending a little time chanting up some courage before I called, he suggested I come and see him that evening after work. Frantically, I called my Auntie Gogi to see if someone could rush Jeff's tape over to my work before my meeting. Obligingly, my mom picked up the tape at my aunt's house and delivered it to me shortly before I left. But, just as the clock struck time to go home, Sy Marsh, Sammy's business manager, called to postpone our meeting. He said something unexpected had come up. *Of course, it did.* His apology sounded sincere, but I was never quite sure if someone was poking a hole in my balloon or if I was being protected somehow. Most of my life, I'd find myself under the mercy of the first choice. But over that last year, the second choice had been popping up more and more.

Wondering why I was so "out of rhythm" after chanting so much for this victory, I dragged myself home, tape in hand. I prepared for an evening pity party while Sy Marsh was out doing whatever had come up. I sat down to chant. When I finished, I turned on my tape player to listen to the tape. Well, what do you know? As I pushed the play button, Jim Croce began to sing *Bad, Bad Leroy Brown*. Oh, man… I could just see how that would have gone down. I would have strolled into Sy Marsh's office saying something like, "Do I have something impressive for you to hear…" Holy mackerel! Protected, AGAIN!

I called my aunt to tell her my mom picked up the wrong tape. She went to check and, yep, Jeff's tape was still in the recorder. Out of curiosity, she asked who my appointment was with, and I told her. She said, "Get outta town! You're kidding me! Sy Marsh managed me for 15 years. Be sure to tell him I said hello." Is there a synonym for WOW?

Much to my surprise, Sy called me the next morning before I had a chance to call him to reschedule. We made an appointment for late that afternoon, but before we hung up, I managed to squeeze in that "Gogi Grant sends her regards". He gushed, "Gogi Grant! She's like my kid sister! I haven't seen her for years! How is she?" He paused, "How do you know Gogi?" Coyly, I replied, "I'm her niece."

"Oh, my god! I can't wait to meet you!"

Well, then it became a family reunion. I didn't really need the tape after all. The happy ending to this phase of my story… Sammy Davis, Jr. found his way to becoming a member on the Board of Directors of Therapeutic Living Centers for the Blind.

∧ ∧ ∧

Unfortunately, Jeff began speaking before the record button was pushed, and his introduction was cut off. I called my aunt again to ask her if he might be able to re-record it. Woefully, she said he was out of town. After a moment of pondering, she suggested she would ask his dad to do it… Lloyd Bridges. Synonym: SENSATIONAL! It did just get better than that! A couple of days later, I had a wonderful tape for Stevie explaining why we wanted him for this most worthy cause… as narrated by Lloyd Bridges. If ever there was a recognizable voice, it would be his. The tape was perfecto, and it will remain a sacred treasure of mine forever.

∧ ∧ ∧

Ever hear about a squeaky wheel? I would call Motown. Ira, Stevie's publicist says Reggie or Chris will call me back. They never do, although they keep promising there will be a meeting. So, I call again and again and again and again. My "hello" becomes voice recognition and Ira and I become phone buddies as our conversations morph into stories about ourselves and life in general.

^ ^ ^

On September 28, 1976, *Songs in the Key of Life* was released. Bill Young called me at work to tell me he had just heard on the radio that Stevie was going to be at Tower Records on Sunset Boulevard at 3:00. Oh man, only about an hour away. I needed to be there! I imagined myself turning green, then slowly walking into King Bob's office. I moaned and groaned that I was sick and needed to go home. You can be sure he didn't want my cooties in his office — so, off I went to Tower Records.

I saw that the parking lot was nearly empty. I went inside and noticed there were only a couple of customers browsing around. Did I have the wrong information? I paced for a while not sure how long I would stay, when a big fancy gold Mercedes pulled up. Three doors opened, and what could easily have been mistaken for the starting lineup of the Rams piled out of the car. I walked over to them and asked if any of them might be the bodyguard who was friends with Herman. Bingo! After being released from the all-time bear hug, the bodyguard morphed into a mother hen and took me under his wing. He told me to stick with him and everything was going to be just fine.

From the time I left the store to go outside and pace, the inside had been cordoned off right across its midsection. The far end from the entry door was Stevie's side along with his entourage. The other side was for everyone else. I got to be on the Stevie side with my mother hen posing as a bodyguard. Stevie and I finally had the opportunity to talk. He knew quite well who I was. Having little to no comprehension of the term, *don't call us, we'll call you*, I suppose has its advantages. After listening to my story, he put his arm around me and pledged to do whatever he could to help us realize this dream. He told me to call and set up an appointment and promised they would sit down with us and come up with a plan of action. He was impressed with this noble project. I gave a big bear hug back to mama bird and floated out on Cloud Nine.

^ ^ ^

As I was about to leave the store, a British woman named Constance Elsner approached me. She said she was writing a biography about Stevie, and by her observation she assumed he and I were friends. She asked if there was a possibility that I might be able to arrange an interview for her. I laughed and told her we were basically wearing the same shoes. She said she was only going to be in town for a couple of days before heading back to London, and she was intrigued to know what Stevie and I were talking about. She invited me to have dinner with her, and we arranged to meet the following evening.

I pulled up in front of a lovely condominium building in West Hollywood. I knocked on the door where she was staying, and a blind man answered. He could have easily doubled for Stevie, and I noticed that behind him on the foyer wall hung a platinum record of *Signed, Sealed, Delivered, I'm Yours* — written by Lee Garrett. Offering his hand, he introduced himself as Lee Garrett and then escorted me into the living room.

After some pleasant conversation with Lee and his girlfriend, Constance and I headed out for dinner. She was lovely. She was also fascinated by my story. I never knew if she was able to get an interview, or if her book was ever published. I thought about it often and I was sorry we lost touch.

Lee and his girlfriend and I became good friends. I introduced them to chanting and I was astounded to find the sutra book that we chant was in braille at the Braille Institute bookstore. I still have my copy.

∧ ∧ ∧

In mid-September, I contacted Herbie Hancock and he was more than pleased to join in our noble cause for Therapeutic Living Centers. We made an appointment to meet with Stevie and his people at my very humble apartment on Camrose Court in the Hollywood Hills. There we all anxiously awaited Stevie's arrival. A couple of hours drifted by, and we surmised Stevie was a no-show. Once Herbie heard the entire saga of TLC, he became even more determined to help us.

"If Stevie won't come to us, we'll go to him."

Bill and I piled into Herbie's car and off we went to the studio. What a night! Stevie greeted us warmly. He listened to Bill's proposal and committed to participate in a benefit concert on behalf of TLC. Bill graciously made his exit… Herbie and I remained. I sat on the end of a piano bench while Herbie and Stevie jammed on keyboards into the wee hours of the morning.

∧ ∧ ∧

As soon as the universe rolled out the red carpet for my great benefit, an amazing chain of events took place. After a long and challenging battle for government funding, TLC finally received approval, allowing the dream to come true without the need for fundraising. The funding was not only to get it off the ground, but for its survival. TLC has provided a stellar quality of life for dozens of multi-handicapped blind adults with many group homes for varying degrees of disability. They have workshops, dance parties and field trips. The residents have been enabled to live as normal of lives as they can. My sister Nancy lived there happily with her boyfriend, Chris, until she passed away in 1996.

∧ ∧ ∧

A couple of years later, I was hosting a Buddhist meeting at my place on Stanley Avenue. One of the members had a guest with her and introduced him during the meeting. His name sounded so familiar. After the meeting, she brought him over to meet me. When he heard my name, (Debbie Torres at the time), he said, "Debbie Torres? I'm Stevie's publicist!" you know, the one I became phone buddies with.

He asked me what I was doing there. I said, "I live here."

He told me there was a book written about Stevie by a woman named Constance Elsner, and that a portion of one of the chapters was about me and my quest for TLC. I made every effort to find a copy of that book, but I never was able to. Perhaps one day it will land on my doorstep!

∧ ∧ ∧

Fast forward 22 years (which happens to be my lucky number) to the year 2000. Three of my girlfriends, who happened to also be co-workers, and I, collectively underwent gastric bypass surgery. Two of us were poster children, while the other two struggled with far too many complications. As one of the poster children, I began receiving referred inquiry calls from people considering their own potential surgeries. I would always Google the Obesity.com site to find the most recent articles to send to people or to share my own success story. One day while in the Century City law firm where I worked, I received a call from a woman curious about bypass surgery. As I always did, I Googled Obesity.com and what popped up on my screen was a list of Stevies: Steven Spielberg, Steven Segal, Stevie Nicks… AND a used copy of Constance Elsner's paperback, *Stevie* for 99¢ on Amazon.com. *WHAT!!! ARE YOU KIDDING ME RIGHT NOW?!?!*

Sometimes I swear its magic!

14

STANLEY AVENUE

In 1976, I was living with two roommates in an average sized one-bedroom apartment on Camrose Court in the Hollywood Hills. In truth, it was barely the first incline up to the Hollywood Hills. Our building sat one notch above a sleaze motel on Highland Avenue, a few blocks from Hollywood Boulevard on one side, and the Hollywood Bowl on the other.

We had a system. Each week we rotated: one in the bed, one on the couch, and one on the floor. I had much grander plans for my living situation. And, after all, I was a novice practitioner of Buddhism, so surely, I had everything I needed to manifest my grandiose vision.

I typed up a list of specifics. The universe must be tested once again! Just how sincere is this universe, anyway? My dream was to live in one of those wonderful neighborhoods filled with turn of the century massive Spanish duplexes. It must be complete with two bedrooms, a large functional kitchen, a formal dining room, a fireplace, a stained-glass window, and be cockroach free. And, naturally, it had to be in my price range… which wasn't very much and wasn't very likely.

My wish list sat on my Buddhist altar for a month as I determinedly chanted for this wish to come true. Day in and day out, I demanded actual proof of my chanting. Day after day nothing happened. As the sun rose on the fourth Saturday of my campaign, I was moping around in defeat, when a friend of mine asked where I had been looking. Looking? Looking for what? Looking for my dream home? No, I hadn't been looking? I'd been chanting for it. Ohhhhh… Buddhism is based on cause and effect? I thought my chanting for it was my cause. I actually have to go out and look for it?! Hmmmm… okay. I got dressed and headed out to see what I might find.

That was at 9:00 in the morning. By 2:30, I had not spied even one For Rent sign. I was getting bored and hungry and cranky. At that point, I was driving around the neighborhood of the Los Angeles County Art Museum (the Wilshire/Fairfax district). I turned the corner on Stanley Avenue, which dead ends at the famous La Brea Tar Pits. Proceeding slowly down the street, I saw some kids playing in the front yard of one of the duplexes. As I rolled by, one of the kids let out a shrill scream. I slammed on my brakes afraid I must have just run over one of them. My heart was pounding as I reluctantly turned my head to see what had happened. Much to my relief, what had happened was that the kids were playing tag and one of them screeched as the tagger caught him.

Breathing in a deep sigh of relief, I noticed that the arched stained-glass window of the lower unit was uncovered revealing an empty interior. No visible signs anywhere. I breathed in deeply, summoning up courage. I pulled over and parked. Stepping onto the lawn I was able to have a better view inside this fabulous vacancy.

Quietly chanting in my ventriloquist fashion, I slowly mounted the stairs to the upper unit and rang the bell. The porch was enclosed with a black wrought iron security gate. A woman about my mother's age poked her nose through the chain locked door. Looking me up and down, she asked me what I wanted. I said I was out looking for a place to rent and it looked like the unit downstairs was empty. She gruffly stated it had already been rented.

Vista Del Mar, a highly respected children's center in Los Angeles was preparing for a benefit luncheon at the elegant Bonaventure Hotel. My Auntie Gogi's performance was to be the main course. I had volunteered to sell tickets, and just happened to have some in my purse.

Before the woman could shut the door on me, I mentioned that Gogi Grant was doing a benefit concert for Vista Del Mar, and that I was selling tickets. Before I could wind up my pitch, she opened the door and said, "GOGI GRANT? I used to date someone who worked in her father's flower shop. I had dinner at her parent's house more than once." I responded in awe, "Ummm… they would be my grandparents."

Now that it had been established that we were practically related, I asked if it would be okay to peek at the downstairs unit so I could get an idea of what you get for your money. She said she'd be happy to show it to me. Her name was Tina.

With key in the lock, and the drum rolling, she pushed the beautiful heavy wood door open. I could feel it. This place was mine!

We stepped into a lovely little foyer that opened into an enormous living room with an old-world-type stone fireplace and mantle, 12-foot arched ceilings, a large stained-glass window exposing the front yard garden with built-in bookshelves on either side of the window. The living room stepped up to a sizable formal dining room that led into a wonderful kitchen adjoining a quaint breakfast room. To the right of the kitchen was a full-sized laundry area, and at the back of the unit were two oversized bedrooms and a lovely art deco bathroom dressed in mint green and black tiles.

She offered to tell me the rent was $325 a month. She also confessed that it had not been rented. She said she didn't want anyone so young renting it, but since we obviously went way back, she thought it was meant to be. We were certainly on the same page with that. I asked if it would be okay to get my roommate and come back a little later.

I drove as fast as my little VW bug could go to fetch Patricia. As we approached the duplex, Tina was coming down the stairs with a young woman. Patricia and the young woman looked at each other in amazement and said, "I know you!" They had been friends in high school. The young woman was Tina's daughter. Well, we just seemed to be related all the way around.

I would later come to find that Tina's birthday was October 4th, the same as my mother, and her husband Richard's birthday was November 10th, the same as my father.

I lived on Stanley Avenue for 11 years. Tremendous Buddhist good fortune would spring forth from that address… including the birth of both of my children.

15

BECOMING
A MOMMY

I had started working at Kaiser Hospital on Sunset Boulevard in 1975, shortly after beginning my Buddhist practice. I had been dating another Buddhist member for some time when I made an appointment to see my doctor to have a pregnancy test. He asked me the standard question, "How late are you?" I explained that I wasn't late. He laughed and sent me on my way, telling me to come back in a couple of months. I made a return visit a week later and insisted he do a test... so he did... and so I was. That was a magnificent, magical, miraculous moment... I WAS GOING TO BE A MOMMY! I was 29 years old and had been told when I was 19 that I would never be able to have children! I WAS GOING TO BE A MOMMY! I was so elated, that for a moment it never occurred to me that anyone else might have been involved.

Having no intention of running the risk of dealing with my own inner weakness by being bullied into another abortion, I decided to break up with the father and keep this treasure to myself. I was on Cloud Nine, and no one was going to take my miracle away from me... NO ONE!

When I was about four months along, one of my friends suggested that it might not be fair for the father to overhear this news at a Buddhist meeting and that I may want to reconsider telling him. Naturally, I had to agree with her. So, I gathered myself, chanted an abundance of Nam-myoho-renge-kyo to wake up my own courage, and then took the plunge. I made it clear that I would never ask him for anything or ever expect anything from him, and he obligingly washed his hands on the whole thing... and I left.

When my daughter was six months old, I felt that her only chance of establishing a relationship with her father would be if I found a way to resolve something with my own biological father. I needed to break this chain of perpetual karma so a new path could be paved for her.

After the incredible encounter I had with the man in the Urology Department a few years earlier, I at least had a starting point. So, I called my father's brother, the optometrist. He told me that he and George had been estranged from each other for years, but he thought their sister in San Diego may know how to reach him.

Out of curiosity, I invited my uncle and his wife to my house for dessert that evening so we could meet. When I opened the door, there stood an uncle, an aunt, three beautiful cousins and a grandmother. It was quite the Kodak Moment. Although it was an unforgettable evening, I still had reservations about getting involved, so we made it a point to exchange Christmas cards and a phone call now and again.

I made the call to my aunt in San Diego. Unfortunately, she also shared with me her estrangement from George, although, they did have one mutual friend who may have known his whereabouts.

One evening about a week later, I received a call from a man who said, "Is this Debbie?" I said it was. And then he announced, "This is your pop."

We talked for hours sharing all the painful details of our lives and how incredibly parallel they ran.

His parents came to America from Greece. My grandfather was a real ladies' man, and not too long after they arrived, my grandfather abandoned my grandmother and my infant father. My peasant grandmother knew she could not remain in this country unless she was married. She also knew she would not be marketable having a child in tow. George's version of the story was that she placed him in an orphanage and not long after, she met Chris Tasulis, Sr., and they married. Two children, Chris, Jr. and Elaine, were born to them. According to George, he remained in the orphanage for five years, his stepfather knowing nothing of his existence. There was a similar version of this story that my Aunt Helen told me many years later, but essentially having the same outcome.

Eventually, according to George, my grandmother finally told her husband about her son, and they brought him home. Cinderella may very well have been modeled after his childhood experience, my own running a close second.

After our initial conversation, every month for seven years my father called with the promise of coming to visit me and my daughter. Although he only lived a couple of hours away in Oceanside, it never happened.

The amazing news was that about four months after my first conversation with George, my daughter's father appeared on my doorstep, on his 30th birthday, to meet her. She was 10 months old. He fell in love with her and eventually we were married. It was a disaster from the start, and we were divorced a couple of years later. Over time… a long time… and chanting abundant Nam-myoho-renge-kyo… we became friends… and I am grateful.

I had remarried in 1985 and was eight months pregnant with my second child by my fourth husband, which was seven years after my first contact with George and approximately 84 no-shows on his part. I received a call from my Uncle Chris telling me that my grandmother had passed away. We hadn't spoken in a while, but I decided to attend the funeral out of respect and my mother decided to accompany me. I had no expectation of my father being there because of their family history.

As we pulled into the Greek Orthodox Church in Los Angeles, I noticed a huddle of men standing in the parking lot. I pointed to one of them and declared, "There's George." My mother insisted it was not. How could I possibly know as I'd only seen him one time. She suggested we go and find out. I knew it was him, but I was not about to make the first move, so I waddled up the steps of the church while she went to investigate. Upon reaching the top of the steps, my three newfound cousins approached me with another beautiful young woman. The introduction nearly induced labor. It went something like this: "Debbie, I want you to meet your sister, Dana."

WOW! And yes, it was George in the parking lot. It's astounding what can happen at a funeral.

Dana's mother, also divorced from George, was with her, so Dana and her mother, and me and my mother spent a perfectly delightful afternoon together with George.

^^^

Approximately 10 years later and divorced from hubby number four, I came home from work one day to find a message on my answering machine. The woman on the other end said she had found my name on the internet and thought that we might be sisters. Her name was Susan and she lived in Medford, Oregon. I called her right away and found that we were indeed sisters, and she had a younger sister named Stephanie. Their mother had been married to George and they too had no relationship with him, but the three of us formed a bit of a bond and have stayed in touch now and again.

George owned a bait and tackle shop on the Oceanside Pier for decades. He had a fishing boat that he frequently took to Mulegé, Baja California Sur, Mexico, where he spent an inordinate amount of time. As sure as I'm sitting here pounding away on the keyboard, I strongly sense that I have many more beautiful Greek/Mexican sisters somewhere. I just may take a trip someday to find them.

^^^

At the New Year of 2009, George had been on mind. I was living in Alaska and was planning to be in California in July when my first grandchild was expected. I thought it might be an opportunity to gather my three sisters and make a surprise visit to see George. If the mountain will not come to Muhammad, then Muhammad must go to the mountain. Unfortunately, I had lost my connections with my sisters, so on the off chance my cousin Christine might know how to reach them, I called her to see if she could help. She had Susan's phone number, but she had no idea how to contact Dana. I called Susan right away and she was thrilled at the idea, and she reached out to Stephanie. I chanted to miraculously locate Dana. A few days later, Christine called me to say how surprised she was that Dana had contacted her after finding her number in a storage box. She was looking for the three of us girls with news that George had passed away and she wanted us to know when the services would be.

So, the George daughters did, in fact, get together to go see their father, albeit in a casket. I suppose that may have been the only comfortable way for him to be with us. While we were in Oceanside for the funeral, we went to visit his bait and tackle shop on the Oceanside Pier. We met the new owner and took lots of photos.

About three years later, after moving back to Los Angeles from Alaska, my Aunt Toni's sister, Roma, came to visit her from San Diego. We were sharing a bottle of wine and schmoozing when Roma told me a crazy tale about my father and his bait and tackle shop. A girlfriend of hers had fallen ill, and Roma had gone to help her. Her friend had a male roommate and he and Roma became fast friends. His brother was having a birthday party and he invited Roma to go with him to the party. In conversation, the brother told Roma that he had a bait and tackle shop on the Oceanside Pier. Roma said she had a sort-of relative whose father had a bait and tackle shop on the Oceanside Pier. As it turned out, George was friends with the brother and gifted him the bait and tackle shop when he retired. Wouldn't you know, he was the fellow we were taking photos with a few years earlier on the pier.

16

TOO CLOSE
FOR COMFORT

One Friday evening in mid-1979, when my daughter was about six months old, I had plans to attend a business meeting and my mom came to sit with her. When I came home she said Lindsay had been a little fussy, but she didn't think there was anything to be concerned about. My daughter was precocious from the day she was born. For example, I was in labor on my birthday, Christmas Eve, but she held out until the 27th having decided that she was not sharing her birthday with anyone! Additional proof of her precociousness would be the fact that she cut her first tooth when she was only four months old. There was no reason to believe that her fussiness could be anything more than another eruption in the works.

Lindsay was quiet all through the night and woke up about 5:15 a.m. Nothing unusual about that except she was a little fussy. Mother's intuition pushed me aside and wrapped her up in a bundle and had me head to the ER. It wasn't like she was writhing in pain. She didn't have a fever. She was not abnormally fussy for a baby cutting a tooth. But I took her anyway.

Shift change in the ER was 6:00 a.m. We arrived about 5:50, just as the ER pediatrician was wrapping up her shift. They could have had us wait for 10 minutes while the new doc geared up, but before the parting doc left, she took Lindsay into an examining room, looked her over and palpated her tummy. Glancing at me with a bit of concern, she said, "I think she has an intussusception." "A what?" I asked.

The pediatrician explained to me that an intussusception is a collapse of the intestine and that the collapsed portion then begins to crawl inside itself — kind of like poking your finger in the bottom of a balloon and pushing it upwards. She offered that it was an extremely rare condition, and that it was also extremely dangerous. She told me that most times a radiologic barium enema generally blows it back out. They would make that attempt three times, but if it didn't work, Lindsay would have to be rushed into surgery and have that portion of her intestine removed or she would die. *Or she would die…*

I was a single mom and all alone. I was in shock. I let them take my baby to x-ray while I remained in the waiting room out of mind with fear. I started to chant with sheer determination for her protection. She had to be sandbagged to keep her still, all the while screaming bloody murder.

After the first attempt, the doctor came out to tell me that that was exactly what was wrong with her, but the enema didn't work. She turned around to go back for round two, as I continued to chant in the waiting room, alone and terrified.

After some time, the doctor came back with the bad news that the second try also failed and that I needed to brace myself for the possibility they may need to rush her into surgery to save her life.

The piercing screams of my baby was too much to bear. I could not control my sobbing, but I continued chanting for her protection.

When the doctor came out the third time, I held my breath until I was nearly ready to pass out. She informed me that it was a success! They were, however, going to keep her for a few days for observation. She also said that had I not listened to my intuition, Lindsay would not be alive to talk about it. The other part of this magical rhythm was, had I arrived at the ER even ten minutes later, a different doctor would have been on duty, and as this condition is so rare, the other doctor may not have even considered that diagnosis.

Bright and early the following Saturday, Lindsay woke up just like she did the prior Saturday morning. Without haste, I bundled her up and rushed to the ER. The doctor on duty, after hearing her history, rushed her into x-ray and came back with a negative report, but he did want to keep her overnight for observation. The next morning, my baby girl had a new tooth.

^^^

My fourth husband John and I had moved back to Lancaster, California in 1988 after my living in Los Angeles since 1970. We opened a Stride Rite Children's Shoe Store, and I pursued real estate. My daughter was nine and our son, Nicholas, was two.

I was in my real estate office when the daycare called to tell me that Nicholas had a rash in his groin area that they thought might be chicken pox — and would I please come and get him. It was about 4:00 o'clock in the afternoon. I called John and asked if he would go and pick him up and that I'd be home shortly. When they got home, John put him in a tepid bath with Epsom salts to hopefully give him some relief. But Nicholas began screaming inconsolably. John called for me to come right away and I dashed home. Nicholas' upper body had a spider-like rash that was spreading rapidly. It most definitely was not chicken pox. We called our doctor and the answering service put us through to him. He was out of state on vacation, but he notified the doctor on-call and told us to get Nicholas to the ER as soon as possible.

The on-call doctor was there ready to take Nicholas in. He walked around the table in deep thought and then said he believed this to be something potentially life-threatening. I asked him what it was, and he became rather condescending as he retorted, "It's complicated and I don't think you'd understand it."

Exasperated, I said, "Try me!"

The doctor proceeded to call for a bed for Nicholas to be admitted. I told him he wasn't going to do anything with Nicholas until he explained to me in detail what the hell he was talking about. Again, he arrogantly stated that it was over my head. I impatiently demanded he explain. He said he believed it was an autoimmune issue. I asked him if he was talking about AIDS. He simply was not going to get into it with me, and I was certainly not going to allow him to have any further contact with my son. I excused myself from the room and put in another call to my doctor as I chanted under my breath for some clarity and protection.

As it turned out, the doctor in the ER was a doctor who was on-call for the doctor who was on-call for the doctor who was on-call. Our doctor had no idea who he was, but he began asking me questions over the phone. From the description of the rash on Nicholas' body, and the vague description from the on-call doc, my doctor asked if I thought Nicholas could tolerate a vehicle transport to Children's Hospital in Los Angeles, or if I thought he was in too much pain and would need to be airlifted. He said it sounded like Henoch Schonlein Purpura (HSP), which is a rare autoimmune disease that affects children. He said that it's the body's reaction to a virus, but it works against itself. What happens is that the veins begin to rupture with tiny pinholes and the patient begins to slowly hemorrhage. If it spreads to the lower part of the body, the kidneys could be permanently damaged and fail to function. Then came words parents do not want to hear — there is no cure — you have to ride it out and hope for the best.

We were able to put a cushy bed together to keep him comfortable in the back of my SUV and I headed to Children's Hospital. My baby cried all the way. I chanted through my tears for absolute strength and complete confidence that he would be okay.

When we arrived, the doctors admitted him immediately and determined that HSP is exactly what he had. The only thing they could do is try to keep him comfortable and observe. It simply had to run its course. We stayed there for four days. I chanted for his protection hours and hours every day. Gradually, it began to disappear. He was discharged and we went home. Our farewell message from the doctors was, "It's never been known to come back. He is good to go. He's a very lucky little guy!"

The doctor who was on-call for the on-call doctor who was on-call happened to be correct in his diagnosis, but unfortunately, he also happened to be someone no parent could possibly trust because of his arrogance. So, we were fortunate he was there, and even more fortunate that our doctor insisted Nicholas be in the care of the best of the best! Thank you, universe!

17

DONNA AND DR. WEINSTEIN

My sister, Donna, suffered her entire life with celiac disease. It seems like she spent more time in the hospital than she did at home enjoying her family. There were many times the disease became so severe that the doctors were not hopeful she would survive the night. Somehow, her stubbornness always pulled her through. I'm certain that's what kept her alive for 61 years. Her normal weight when she was healthy was about 90 pounds… soaking wet. When she became critical, it wasn't uncommon for her to drop down to 70 pounds in a matter of days.

In the late 1990s, Donna and her family lived in the Las Vegas area when her illness had taken a major turn for the worse. The attacks came in greater frequency, and they were harshly more severe. She would barely be over the hump of one, weak and malnourished, when another would strike. She was in and out of the hospital constantly.

One day, as Donna lay in critical condition in the ICU, before she was put on life support, Donna said she dreamed of a time there would be an intestinal transplant available.

It wasn't the first time we had been told she most likely wouldn't make it through the night. And it wasn't the first time our family gathered around her bed hoping and praying it wasn't to say goodbye.

Out of curiosity, I called the Gastroenterology Department at UCLA to see if such a transplant existed. The person I spoke with referred me to a woman who was the head of the Celiac Foundation. The Celiac Foundation? Although it had been in existence for forty years, no one ever mentioned it to us. As it happened, it was an inexhaustible wealth of information… vital information.

After a long discussion with the woman at the Foundation about Donna's declining health, she referred me to Dr. Weinstein at UCLA. He not only was the head of the Gastroenterology Department, but he was the world-renowned specialist in celiac disease.

My conversation with Dr. Weinstein was nothing less than a miracle. He wanted Donna transported to UCLA immediately. After my Aunt Toni and I put our heads together, we found a medical transport to get her to UCLA. Naturally, because her condition was so fragile, it was against the medical advice of the Las Vegas team. All I could do was continue chanting that nothing would go wrong during the long road trip.

Dr. Weinstein was there to admit her. Upon his initial exam, he discovered a malignant tumor in her intestine. How many Las Vegas doctors tried to figure out why, over and above the celiac, she was so sick? They kept coming up empty. The universe certainly bestowed her with great good fortune to meet Dr. Weinstein.

In all his worldwide travels as a specialist, author, professor, lecturer, and researcher, Dr. Weinstein had never seen a celiac case as severe as Donna's. He became her specialist and friend until his retirement years later. But even then, he remained available to her any time she needed.

Eventually it became necessary for Donna to have daily infusions of something called total parenteral nutrition (TPN), which kept her body replenished with nourishment. The cost of one bag of TPN was $1000, and she needed to have it every day to stay alive. There were many roadblocks to getting her insurance coverage, but after fighting tooth and nail, it finally came through. Her vascular system was shot to hell because of the necessary excessive overuse during her lifetime. Since the TPN could not be administered through an IV, it was necessary to have a port-a-cath surgically implanted. The port would eventually clot off and become infected, so they would have to find another location to implant a new one. At one point the doctors surgically implanted one at her heart… it was her last resort. They said it was extremely risky and didn't know how long it might last.

Donna was in and out of the hospital more times than I can count. Sometimes it was for a couple of days and other times it was up to six or eight weeks. The fact that it was predicted early on that she wouldn't live past 30, it was a miracle that we got to enjoy her until she was 61.

Although she was not a practicing Buddhist, she did occasionally go to meetings with me, and she enjoyed them tremendously. She did chant her way through some pretty, hairy situations though. Nam-myho-renge-kyo cut a pathway of protection for my sister which she so often needed. She had an uncanny stubbornness and I know that stubborn determination is what kept her here for so long. She would be on her last leg, crawl out of a hospital bed and drive from Las Vegas to Los Angeles so she wouldn't miss a Hanukkah party or a birthday party or Thanksgiving. She showed up for everything no matter what! Her sheer determination to *be* was unmatched… except for our mom. They were cut from the same mold.

At the end, I sat on the hospital bed beside her. Donna asked me to hold her hands and chant with her until she slipped away. Nam-myoho-renge-kyo were her last words.

18

THE TREE
OF LIFE

My adoptive father passed away in January of 1981. Although our relationship, at best, was nothing less than a perfect storm, he was the only father I ever knew. Interestingly, that all changed as I was about to become a mother… single and unwed. In fact, he chose her name. From the moment I conceived, all educated and uneducated guesses were that the baby was a boy… definitely a boy… declared absolute by the heart rate, how I carried the baby, yada yada, yada. It was a boy! So, from day one, this child would have the name Ryan.

On the day I went into labor, the hospital put me on a fetal monitor and the nurse proudly exclaimed, "I've been doing this for 30 years, and I have NEVER been wrong. This baby is without a doubt a boy."

They sent me home twice because I wasn't dilated enough. So, before our third and final trip to the hospital, my dad said, "What if it's a girl?" And I said, "But it isn't!" And he said, "But what if it is? You might want to have a backup name, just on the off chance…"

So, as I sat uncomfortably on the sofa watching little fists and feet, and oh, yes, the tush push kick and poke, we scoured a book of baby names. I liked the name Devlyn. I thought it was lovely, but my parents convinced me that she would be teased all her life and be called a little devil. Then my dad reminded me of my inexhaustible addiction to Greek olives during my pregnancy and suggested I call her "Lindsay" with the hope of becoming heir(ess) to the olive empire. Hey, why not… it didn't really matter… she was a BOY!

Well, after 36 hours of hard labor and wishing I was dead, the second that baby popped out, I insisted I must be in the wrong delivery room as they shouted out, "IT'S A GIRL!"

During this miraculous advent into the world, something deeply transformed in my dad. He fell in love with my baby "Lindsay." But that wasn't all, I also transformed my relationship with him. Buddhism says that when you sincerely chant Nam-myoho-renge-kyo, the transformation that occurs within, is reflected in your environment in kind. I spent a lot of time and energy at my altar seeking to understand all the pain from my childhood and what I had done to make him treat me the way he did. It was between the time I announced I was going to have a baby and shortly before he passed away that I realized how deeply he suffered after my mom's accident. He was a young man. He had a severely damaged wife and two severely damaged children. How could he have known what he signed up for? And then there I was, the only healthy one (except for the asthma) who wasn't even really his. The surfacing of that profound realization was when our relationship blossomed.

Six months after his passing, the international president of the Buddhist organization, SGI-USA, was coming from Japan to visit the United States. During his time in Southern California, many events were being scheduled… all of them by invitation only. Although hundreds of people would attend, they were managed with an incredible degree of precision, and rarely were exceptions made to the rules. Of course, in Buddhism, it also, ALWAYS depends on the sheer determination of the practitioner. So, the reality is, nothing is impossible!

One of the events, a celebration of song and dance was to be held on a Monday at our center in Malibu. The guest list was comprised of two people from each district from all over the western states. I was fortunate enough to have been one of the members selected. The problem was, I had been out of work for a week with bronchial pneumonia, and my first day back to work just happened to fall on that day. I feared that if I missed one more day, I might lose my job. So, I declined the opportunity and returned my ticket.

Naturally, having made such a rash decision without having chanted about it first, once that light bulb went on, I realized the opportunity I was passing up. I immediately called my Buddhist leader, Koko, to tell her I had made a terrible mistake and changed my mind. She apologized profusely telling me she had given the ticket to another member and there simply was no way to change it.

After I finished kicking myself in the derriere, I sat down and single-mindedly chanted that I could somehow turn the situation around. This was not an opportunity to throw away. There must be a reason why I had been selected in the first place. It was an opportunity to fight for.

On the eve of the event, my daughter became so fussy the only way I could calm her down was to put her in her car seat and drive around until she fell asleep. I had been weaving through residential neighborhoods in Los Angeles for about an hour. I was about five miles from my home when the person in the car behind me began impatiently honking their horn. The rudeness of the driver was so annoying, and I pulled over to let the car go by. But it pulled up behind me. It was dark outside and that made me a bit uneasy, so I started chanting that nothing was going to happen. Suddenly, the driver jumped out of the car and ran up to my door. It was Koko. She had tears streaming down her face as she waved a ticket at me. She had been volunteering at the culture center in Santa Monica when someone arrived from Orange County with an extra ticket.

Koko had been sitting on the step at my house waiting for me for an hour when she decided to leave and somehow ended up behind me… nowhere near either of our homes.

Early in the morning I called in sick for one more day and then headed to the community center in North Hollywood where members were boarding buses to attend the Malibu activity. A young man holding a clipboard was checking names off the list. If your name was not on the list, you did not get on the bus. Of course, my name was not on the list. Luckily, one of our leaders was standing behind me and assured the list keeper that it was okay for me to board. He reluctantly acquiesced.

When we arrived in Malibu, there were busloads of people from all over the western states lined up to go inside. If your name was not on the list at the gate, YOU DID NOT GET IN! My name was not on the list. Again, the same leader who had approved me to board the bus, vouched for me once again. But this time the keeper of the gate was not about to breach his duty. HE WOULD NOT LET ME

IN! I waited until every, last bus was unloaded, and every, last person was checked in. I suppose he was feeling sorry for me as he approached and said he thought it would be okay for me to go inside.

The grounds were gorgeous. A few circus-sized canopies had been set up with rows of several hundred chairs. As I wandered around searching for a chair, I found that none were unoccupied. On a beautifully manicured lawn just to the right of the canopies sat a lovely gazebo. I sauntered over and made my place on the grass at its foot.

As I enjoyed my lunch, a Japanese woman came over to me, and in very broken English attempted to ask me a question. She made several attempts, but I just could not quite decipher her message, so she walked away. I noticed her talking to some other people, and out of curiosity, I approached her to give it one more try. This time, I understood her to say she was looking for someone who had recently lost a parent. Curiously, I told her that my father had just passed away, and she exclaimed, "Come with me! Sensei wants to see you right away!" I followed her to another area… a lovely garden with beautiful trees overlooking the ocean. Five of us sat waiting in the garden. Soon, President Ikeda joined us. He said (with the assistance of an interpreter) that we were going to plant trees in honor and memory of our deceased parents - the Flower of Mother and the Flower of Father. Planting a tree of life alongside of President Ikeda in honor of my father was overwhelming. We spent the entire afternoon with President Ikeda, listening to stories and guidance to enrich our lives.

It's so often difficult to remember from experience-to-experience what choices we have, but there are only two… victory or defeat. I knew by the difficulty I had even getting in the gate that I was there for a purpose. This was a gift from my father, the one I suffered with for so many years. But because I never gave up, I was able to change our poison into medicine. For my sake and for the sake of my daughter, I was able to break the shackles of generational karma so she might have a wonderful life experience with her own father. I have such deep appreciation for the never ending treasures that enrich my life.

19

ISCHEMIC COLITIS

In 2002, my mom was transported by paramedics to Kaiser Permanente Hospital in Panorama City. My sisters and I followed her into the emergency room. She was in excruciating pain and out of her mind with confusion. I had never witnessed such fear in anyone's eyes. She grabbed my hands just as she was being rushed into surgery, and cried, "I am so afraid!" Those were the last words I heard her speak.

In dribs and drabs, my enormous family arrived in the waiting room. I sat quietly chanting to myself for a miracle while the others paced the room or quietly talked. Finally, the surgeon came out. It was evident that the news he was about to bare was not going to be good. In laymen's terms, he described as best he could that what she had was like an aneurysm of the colon... it burst — it's called ischemic colitis. All but a few inches of her colon had been removed and her body had been overcome with infection and she was toxic. Only time would tell if she would pull through.

We spent the next three months on a roller coaster — the kind that scares the hell out of you and no matter how brave or strong you might be, you land with your heart in your stomach. Mom remained comatose and on full life support for the duration. My family became permanent fixtures in the halls and waiting rooms of KPMG. We spent untold hours swept away in our thoughts, our fears, our lives, her life. We cried. We laughed. We meditated. We shared memories.

At the time, I was working in a Century City law firm where my commute was easily an hour and a half one way. I spent that time on the standstill freeway chanting

Nam-myoho-renge-kyo. After work, every day, I went directly to the hospital. I spent weekends sitting by her bed waiting for something to happen… anything. Even with all that powerful energy enveloping my life, I was constantly grappling to hold onto hope.

Her condition never altered unless it was spiraling downward, which it did on more than one occasion. Fortunately, the indescribable rhythm that was manifesting in my life always had me on the scene when something went wrong.

At one point, both of her kidneys shut down and she was put on daily dialysis. The nephrologist told us that dialysis could only sustain kidney function for so long before her body would simply reject it. We had also been told that even if she did come out of the coma, which by then was highly unlikely, her kidneys would be useless.

One afternoon I followed my mom's transport into dialysis to sit with her as the machine mimicked the function of her kidneys. I was not supposed to be in there.

Aside from one nurse, my mom and I were the only other people in the room. The nurse sat at a desk about 20 feet from where my mom's blood was being exchanged with her back to us thumbing through a magazine. In an instant, my mother turned blue. I called out to the nurse for help and without skipping a page-turning beat, she huffed, "That's why you aren't supposed to be in here! She's fine!" I retorted, "I said she is blue!" The nurse was apparently too absorbed in some recipe, or a new hairdo to bother turning around. Mercilessly, I raised my voice, "If you don't get over here right now and call for help, you will not have a job this afternoon!" She stood and turned around ready for the fight until she laid eyes on my mom and called a Code Blue. The room instantaneously filled with a team of doctors and nurses. The chaos was crushing, and I didn't know what to do with myself. I started chanting through my fear of losing her right then and there. I was barely able to breathe. Astonishingly, they were able to revive her, and she was rushed to ICU. Had one more moment passed, she would have died. My life was in perfect alignment with hers. I cried tears of appreciation all the way home.

Even though she was comatose and on life support, I did my best to fill her surroundings with things she loved… music, and laughter. They say that people in a coma can hear what's going on, and I know music can move mountains, so I'd put her favorite Big Band tunes on and sing and dance around the room. I believed if she could hear it, she'd be dancing with me.

One day when I was hanging out with mom playing music, I noticed her eyelids were about a quarter open (I think they always were). It was just enough to see her beautiful green eyes, but on that day, I glanced over at her and noticed the whites of her eyes were yolk yellow and so was her skin. I called the nurse who came in right away. In my humble opinion, her response was not the right one, as she matter-of-factly went on to say, "The doctors already made their rounds this morning, and if they thought there was anything to be concerned about, they would have given me orders." Shuddering at her reply, I said, "This isn't this morning, and I've been here for quite a while, and this just happened! You need to get a doctor in here right now." She said there were no doctors in the station, and it would have to wait until the evening rounds. My outrage was getting the better of me, and I resorted to my new old standby, "If you don't get a doctor in here right now, you will not have a job this afternoon!" She huffed on her way out of the room, and I began to chant with all my heart. Within a few minutes, the ER doctor arrived with nurses in tow. He took one look at her and called for an emergency transport to surgery. Family was always around running in different shifts, and I was so grateful some of them were there that day.

When the doctor came out of surgery, he said she was one lucky lady. They discovered that the liver valve collapsed, and poison was streaming into her blood. They had inserted a stint in the liver for the valve to operate. He said that had she not been rushed into surgery right then and there she would not have made it. Then he added, "She is a very sick lady, and she has a long way to go before she's out of the woods. All we can do is wait and see."

We did our best to have someone with her at the hospital as much as humanly possible.

About two months in, the pulmonologist explained that mom could not remain on a ventilator indefinitely, and although there were brainwaves, she wasn't doing anything else on her own. The damage to her body and brain from the toxicity and her kidney failure, made it unlikely she would ever recover. He told us the best we could hope for, if she was removed from the ventilator, would be that she would remain in a vegetative state for however long she might last. Then he suggested we seriously consider shutting down the machines and let her go. Those words were like a sucker punch in the gut and then being kicked while you're down for the count.

For the better part of my life, my mom and I walked a tumultuous tightrope. The resentment I harbored for her, and my dad, ran through a deep cavernous river. I was well into my 40's when we found our way to the beginnings of a respectful relationship, but my true moment blossomed that day as I sat gazing deeply into her vacant green eyes. For the first time, I felt her pain. Her bravery. Her massive losses and disappointments. Her phenomenal victories! Her love… and her life. I could not contain my sorrow. How cruel that this would be the finale. We hadn't even started yet.

My family was shaken to the core. It was getting late, and we all needed to eat. My sisters, my daughter, my niece, and I went to a Japanese restaurant we frequented. On our way to the restaurant, Rod Stewart began to sing *For the First Time*. I sobbed from a place I didn't know existed.

Before we went in, we indulged in a much-needed distraction and smoked a bit of funny stuff. I doubt any of us could have survived that evening without it, and it turned out to be the best medicine. We ordered a drink and edamame was served hot and salty as we waited for our meals. Quietly absorbed in our thoughts we devoured the edamame. My sister said with pod in hand, "Why are all mine empty?" Our collective delayed reactions as we pondered her dilemma resulted in simultaneous uncontrollable laughter. We were so loud, we nearly got kicked out of that respectable establishment. My sister being the only one whose lightbulb hadn't gone off yet, made it that much more hilarious. She had been dipping into the bowl of discards, chewing on each one individually, to no avail. The universe had our backs that evening.

As I lay in bed that night tossing and turning soaking my pillow in tears, I could hear my mom telling us multitudes of times that should anything ever happen to her, *she did not want to be kept alive on machines. Her wishes were to be set free.* And now we were being faced with that dreadful decision. Buckets of heartbreak poured out of me. I chanted for hours for the wisdom and courage to do the right thing. Her fate was in our hands. Shouldn't we honor her wishes? What if we made the wrong choice?

We met at the hospital the next day. None of us wanted to have that conversation. I painfully suggested that we consider mom's wishes. My sisters were not willing to do that, and I was not going to fight against the majority. So, we collectively refused to turn off the machines.

The primary care doc had fallen in love with our great big animated family. He met us in the waiting room nearly every day just to visit and soak us up. He was a smart, attentive, cuddly, funny, warm human. He told my sisters and me that he was going to retire after the first of the year, and it was his wish, that if she recovered, he wanted nothing more than to have a dance with her at his celebration party.

Mom was eventually taken off life support, and miraculously she continued breathing on her own. As weeks drifted by, her kidneys began to function on their own. And then one day, she woke up. The beginning of her arduous recovery had begun.

A few months later, my sister Donna and I wheeled mom up the plank and into the restaurant where the doc's retirement party was being held. We parked ourselves at one of the tables out of the way so mom could remain in the wheelchair. After a few announcements and lots of applause for the doc, he lifted mom to a wobbly standing position as he held her close so she wouldn't fall, and they slow danced to the first song of the evening.

20

NANA AND THE FAIRYTALE WARRIOR

In 1975 I joined the chorus in our Buddhist group. All the youth members gathered on Sunday mornings at our center on the beach in Santa Monica to chant together and then disburse outside for practice — drill team, fife and drum corps, young men's brass band and orchestra, and the chorus. My guess would be there were a few hundred of us, everyone dressed in white shirts and pants.

The first time I went to one of these gatherings, I sat at the back of the room amongst a sea of young chanters. During the chanting, my attention was drawn to a young woman up in the front of the room. All I could see of her was her long corn silk blonde hair. But something drew me into her energy. It was almost like an out-of-body experience. Then during the practice, I got a glimpse of her penetrating blue eyes. It would be quite some time before we would meet, but in the meantime, I wrote a poem about that experience.

A bit later, I attended another Buddhist meeting with about 200 people at our community center in North Hollywood. I had a similar occurrence with a man who sat near the front of the room. Again, it was just a feeling… a kind of knowing. After the meeting, I pointed him out to my cousin and asked if she knew who he was. She said his name was Dan. We never met and I don't remember that I ever saw him again.

The Buddhist organization I practice with is an international peace movement called SGI-USA. Worldwide, members meet primarily in small groups in homes to chant together, share experiences, and learn about the humanistic teachings of Nichiren Daishonin, the 13th century founder of the Buddhism I practice. One of the members in the district group where I practiced was named John. After a year or so, our district group became two smaller districts. I went with the new group while John remained with the original one.

Sometime later I received a phone call from Dan. He said, "You probably don't know who I am, but I wanted to know if you'd like to go to a movie?" I told him that I did know who he was, and I'd be happy to go. We started seeing each other and one day he invited me over for dinner. Much to my surprise, John was there with his new wife, Nana, who just happened to be the woman I was mystically drawn to at my first youth gathering.

Dan and I would marry in the future, a story for another time. Nana, John, Dan, and I became a fabulous foursome. In fact, after Dan and I were married, Nana and John came to live with us temporarily.

In 1981, tremendous turmoil swept over my life, and I lost touch with Nana and John… and, as usual… with myself. Nearly 20 years passed, when in July of 1998, I experienced the incredible intricacies of my universal web. This connection was not born from the internet, but from the weaving of my own karmic relationships which have known no boundaries in time or space.

I had just joined the Columbia House CD Club and received my first shipment of 10 CDs. Two of them were Fleetwood Mac and Boz Skaggs. I selected those two CDs for my long commute to and from work.

For more than a year, I found myself mesmerized by one of the messengers out in the plaza where I worked. He was there nearly every lunch hour. His presence had such a hold on some part of my being, and I would find my mind wandering off into another land… another time. He had long silver hair that flowed down the middle of his back. Blousy shirts and leather pants with knee high boots made him look like a swashbuckling pirate. His face resembled Paul Newman's and his persona was so animated as he entertained his buddies on the plaza. Although I couldn't hear his words, I knew what he was saying. And although I couldn't witness his life, I knew who he was. He was a Fairytale Warrior!

On July 7, I was scouting for an empty seat on the plaza to have lunch, when two fellows rose to leave. I hurried to make a claim on the table. One of them said their friend had left his helmet and they weren't sure where he had gone. I told them I would be there for an hour and would be happy to look after it.

A few minutes later, the Fairytale Warrior approached my table to collect his helmet. How amazing that it would belong to him. He asked if he might join me, and we proceeded to engage in a magical dialogue about life and the universe. The poetry that flowed from his life was not unlike anything I had already imagined about him, but he still took my breath away.

That night a poem flowed from my pen as if someone else had taken charge of my hand. Conjuring up creative inspiration had laid dormant for a very long time. The next day I found him on the plaza and gave him a copy of my poem, then walked away. I observed from a distance as he read. His face lit up like a beacon. When he finished, he looked around to find me. He said he could not believe I saw him as I did… I had captured the essence of his being.

At lunchtime the next day he presented me with a book of his poetry to take home and read. As I turned the pages, I felt my creativity begin to rekindle. That night I desperately tore through my house looking for my old writings. My frustration mounted as I dug through bookcase after bookcase and piles of papers and files in my closet. I could not find them anywhere. In complete exasperation, I found my way to the garage and began digging through boxes that had remained sealed for nearly a decade. Eureka! I found them! I ran back upstairs and opened the box. The first sheet of dusty, wrinkled paper was titled, *The Birth of an Angel.* It was a poem I had written long ago about my old friend, Nana. As I sat there reminiscing, I ached from a deep place in my heart… but it was a cleansing. I spent hours reading poetry I'd written in another lifetime… so many memories.

First thing the next morning, Caryn, the newest secretary in our office, said she had an extra ticket to the Stevie Nicks/Boz Skaggs concert at the Universal Amphitheater for that evening. I must add here that John, of John and Nana, is Stevie's cousin. I could not afford the ticket, but had I gone, the amazing events that followed would never have happened. The synchronicity of that combination of artists performing at the concert, and it being Stevie Nicks, brought me closer to my desire to find Nana.

Amber, another woman in our office bought the ticket from Caryn. The following morning as Amber walked by my desk, I stopped her to ask about the concert. She said it was wonderful, and I matter-of-factly threw in that Stevie's cousin used to live with me. Her jaw dropped as she responded, "Nana?" Then my jaw dropped as I whispered in disbelief, "There is just no way in the world you could possibly know Nana." Amber told me Nana had been the receptionist in our office about 10 years earlier. Mon Dieu! What are the chances of that? My need to find her grew tenfold. I made a phone call to the only person I thought may know how to find her… my ex-husband Dan. The last he had heard John and Nana had split up and John had moved to Arizona.

I called Arizona information and was given three listings for the name Nicks. I called the first number and left a message introducing myself, stating that I was looking for John (not knowing if I had reached the right party). John called me that night. He told me he and Nana had been divorced for several years but he did have a number in Ohio he thought was still hers.

I called and although it was a male's voice on the answering machine, I left a message anyway. Nana returned my call right away. She said she had been in such a dark place and then added that the sound of my voice jarred her, at least for the moment, out of that darkness. I know she had that effect on my life many years before.

The next day when I was at lunch, the Fairytale Warrior joined me and pulled a copy of *The Celestine Vision* out of his bag and shared the profound spiritual experience he had had with that book. I had just finished reading *The Celestine Prophecy* that my old friend and former co-worker Gia had insisted I read years before. As I read it, I couldn't help but reminisce about her. She said that book reminded her of my life, and she couldn't believe I hadn't already devoured it. I felt like the author had fictionalized my story.

Then the Fairytale Warrior mentioned that his band was playing on Friday night at Scruffy O'Shea's, a pub in Venice, and invited me to come.

As I descended on the escalator after work that evening to the underground parking, I spied a woman several steps ahead of me, who from the back, looked like Gia. I called her name and she turned around. We moved ourselves out of the way and did a short catching up. She had just started working in my building that day. I invited her to be my date on Friday and she excitedly accepted, suggesting we go for dinner at Froggie's in Malibu first. There was a gorgeous creature who worked there, and she enjoyed the eye candy. As it turned out, with Friday night traffic, there would not have been enough time, so we went directly to the pub.

We arrived about an hour early and sat out on the patio for a drink when the Fairytale Warrior came to sit with us. In short order, a gorgeous creature walked up to our table to talk to the Fairytale Warrior. Gia looked at him in amazement and then he greeted her with familiarity asking what she was doing there. She nervously stammered that she had come with me to see the Fairytale Warrior's band play. He told her he was the guitarist in the band. Yes, of course, he was the guy from Froggie's. There were four members of the band who had come from a small village in England to pursue their music career in America. They were called Persons Unknown. My Fairytale Warrior and I remained friends up until I moved to Alaska in 2004.

∧∧∧

Mid-June of 1999, my sister Donna, who was living in Las Vegas, called me. She was working in a medical clinic and had become close friends with one of the doctors, an East Indian woman who incorporated alternative and preventive holistic methods of healing into her medical practice. My sister, having been ill most of her life, began using some suggested products recommended by the doctor, and her health was showing some signs of improvement. The doctor had a trip planned to Los Angeles and we arranged for her and her two companions to visit me the evening of June 22.

So, here were these three strangers, from another state, in my living room, talking about alternative medicine with my son and me. Mike introduced himself and continued with sharing his UCLA education and becoming a licensed chiropractor. He had also studied in Japan for many years in the art of alternative healing and preventive medicine. For quite some time he traveled with rock bands on tour as a massage therapist. Only because it was so fresh in my mind, I had to ask, "You mean like Stevie Nicks?" Being thrown for a loop just a tad, he responded, "As a matter of fact, I lived in her house for more than two years. She is the only client I ever had that kind of long-term relationship with." The next comment naturally would be, "So, does that mean you know her cousin, John and his ex-wife Nana?" If you've been following the line of these stories, I am guessing I don't need to answer that, right?

21

THE TRIAL

M y mom was a social butterfly and loved to entertain. She was a humorist, an avid reader, and an engaging conversationalist. As she aged, she had increased difficulty with mobility due to her injuries from the car accident in 1956. Although she was in complete possession of her faculties, in April of 2012, it became necessary for her to reside in a skilled nursing facility for her day-to-day care.

When my mother was in her early teens, she had her thyroid surgically removed. We cannot survive without our thyroid — it controls our brain function, our muscle function, our organs, and our metabolism. Technically, it is the most important organ in our body.

A little more than a year into her living at the nursing home, she was hospitalized for pneumonia. Upon readmission to the nursing home a few days later, for some unknown reason, her thyroid medication had been inadvertently omitted for her readmission, even though it was included in the hospital discharge summary, not to mention the fact that every single page of her nursing home records documented her diagnosis of hypothyroidism and her necessary medication.

She began to decline rapidly and became extremely confused, she didn't want to eat, her body was abnormally swollen, she was in agonizing pain, she cried all the time, and when she wasn't crying, she slept. My sisters and I had no idea what was happening to her other than wondering if it just might be her time. Watching her suffer like that was unbearable. We felt so helpless. I chanted for hours for her suffering to go away.

After four months of this decline, her condition became so dire that she was admitted to the hospital at the end of October 2013. Her primary care doctor never returned a call from the hospital or the nursing home, and he never showed up to see her. The admitting doctor began running tests to figure out what was going on and found that her thyroid level was at zero. He couldn't believe she was even alive. When we asked how that was possible since she had been on thyroid medication all her life, he said she could not possibly have been on her medication for at least the past three to four months for it to have fallen to where it was. He said that was why she was in such agonizing pain — her muscles were breaking down and her organs were systematically failing. We were dumbfounded!

We fired her doctor and chose to have the hospitalist be solely in charge of her care. Because her condition was so fragile, the hospitalist ordered that she NOT be given any narcotics for pain as it would push her over the edge. That night, the same nurse, against the hospitalist's orders, called the doctor we had fired. We later learned that although he was listed in all her records as her primary care, he had never met her, and having no idea why she was in the hospital, he ordered Norco, a heavy-duty narcotic for pain. Hours later, my mom was rushed to ICU and put on life support. The hospitalist was outraged by his actions.

We were enveloped in total chaos. It was shocking to feel how deeply and violent my rage ran. The intensity of my chanting seemed to fan the fire, but I battled on having no idea what we would be coming up against.

My mentor, Daisaku Ikeda says, "When you live to fulfill your great mission and actualize your belief in what is right and true, you will face any manner of trials. You may even experience unreasonable opposition or pressure. No matter what difficulties you meet, however, you can fearlessly and boldly resolve to face them head-on and overcome them without fail. The power of Nam-myo-ho-renge-kyo will surely lead you to bring forth the 'heart of a lion king,' the invincible bravery of a Buddha." I could not possibly fathom the meaning of this at that time.

I called the Los Angeles County Ombudsman and requested that they do an investigation of my mom's medical records. Upon their completion, a damning complaint was filed with the Department of Justice for criminal actions, the Department of Health against the nursing home, the California Medical Board against the doctor, and the licensing board against the nurse practitioner.

My mom remained in ICU on life support until November 17, 2013, when she peacefully passed away surrounded by her family. Our family karma runs deep, as four other members of our family lost their lives to medical malpractice… a 21year-old cousin, a sister at 40, a cousin at 42, and one of my uncles.

Through this endless heartbreak, I vowed through my chanting that if my mom had to die such a horrific death, it would have been for a noble cause! I decided I would not sit idly by but would take courageous action to right this atrocious wrong. It took months before I could bring myself to search for an attorney, but when I did, I landed the best possible find for our cause.

It was explained to us that California has a cap on malpractice of $250,000 regardless of how many defendants there are. It was also explained that elder abuse is nearly impossible to prove as egregious behavior must be established, and most of the time, it simply winds down to an "oopsie"… a mere oversight. But we initiated a wrongful death/elder abuse lawsuit naming one doctor, a nurse practitioner, the nursing home, and the pharmacologist.

My determination from the beginning was that somehow our case would set a precedent in the policies and procedures that govern nursing home care. My purpose was not to take a nuisance settlement and brush this under the carpet so these wrongdoers could continue destroying lives with no consequence. I placed a card on my Buddhist altar that read: "TRUTH & JUSTICE!" — PROFOUND, UNFATHOMABLE, UNPRECEDENTED, IMMEASURABLE, EXTRAORDINARY VICTORY — WITHOUT FAIL!"

During the first year and a half of this lawsuit, we participated in two mediations. Not one defendant came to the table with an offer during the first round. The second time, we were offered $100,000 for a global settlement. My attorney packed up his briefcase and we walked out. I told him that I believed this case was going to put him on the map. He agreed we had a strong case, but stated we needed to focus on the malpractice aspect because the elder abuse would be so difficult to prove. I had every confidence that if anyone could prove it, he would.

I had been working for an attorney in Santa Monica when we were offered the global settlement of $100,000. He strongly suggested it would be foolish for us not to take that money and run, insisting that settlements are calculated by the age of the plaintiff and their potential future economic contributions to family and society. Reminding me that my mom lived in a nursing home and was 81 years old, she essentially had no monetary value as a human being. I was so disheartened by his words, but looked him in the eye and said, "Watch me!"

Because of my litigation background, I had the rare opportunity to work as a team member with our attorney. As the case progressed, I discovered a signature in the nursing home records that was assumed belonged to a nurse. Out of curiosity I Googled the name and found it to be an "employee" doctor of the primary care. After a little digging, we came to find that she was the one assigned to all nursing home rounds. We brought her into the case and during her deposition, she openly admitted abandoning my mom's care for 10 months stating her reasoning was that nursing home visits weren't cost effective — she made more money seeing patients in the clinic. Then she admitted falsifying all those months of medical records nine months after my mom's death when she was named a defendant in the case. They certainly took no issue with fraudulently collecting Medicare payments for those months even though there were no patient visits.

Despite the $250,000 cap on malpractice per case, not per defendant, the "employer" doctor, whose name was listed in all my mom's records but who never saw her, settled for his malpractice policy limit of $1 million. The nursing home, who was self-insured, settled for $1.5 million, and the pharmacologist settled for what we felt was reasonable for his contribution to her death. It is customary that defendants demand a "confidentiality clause" in settlements such as these to disallow any, and all, discussions about the case and the settlements, which they did. But we refused to settle with that clause in place, stating we had every intention of using this case to fight for change… all three of them removed the clause from their agreements.

We were still waiting on the worst of the offenders to settle — the employee doctor.

At the trial setting conference, the judge asked the defendant's attorney how we were doing on settlement negotiations. Her counsel cockily stated, "We are about as far apart in negotiations as the sun is to the moon, Your Honor." The judge classically glared at him over his glasses and said, "Isn't your client the one who falsified all those medical records… and that's okay with you?!" Trial was set for June 2, 2018.

In the interim, my attorney was contacted by two Senior Journalists from CNN. They were working on a series regarding elder abuse in nursing homes and asked permission to interview me. We provided them with her medical records, court documents, and damning deposition transcripts for their reference. The article was published. We were also contacted by The American Association for Justice (AAJ), a national group of lobbying attorneys who fight the big fights for human and civil rights. Their topic of discussion during the interview was HR1215, a piece of legislation initiated by House Representative Steve King from Iowa. That legislation was so deeply sinister, if passed, it would result in there being little to no accountability of doctors, nurses, hospitals, nursing homes, pharmaceutical companies, and device manufacturers in cases of malpractice, abuse, elder abuse, violence, sexual assault, device failures, and rape against patients. The AAJ asked that after the bill passed the House, which it did, and should the Senate allow hearings before a vote, would I be willing to testify before Congress to share my mom's experience. It has yet to hit the Senate floor.

We lost my sister Donna on St. Patrick's Day, three days before her 61st birthday and just three months before our scheduled month-long trial. The shocking heartbreak of her untimely death and the anxiety we faced for the upcoming trial pushed us all over the emotional cliff.

Then, as opening arguments commenced, the building where I had lived for six years had been evacuated and red tagged for negligent asbestos contamination. The entire street was barricaded and lined with fire engines, police cars, news media trucks, and every government agency imaginable. None of the tenants were allowed to retrieve their belongings, and vehicles were not allowed to be removed from the carport. Tenants were hosed down in the alley by Hazmat, scrubs and booties were handed out by the Red Cross along with hotel vouchers and money for food. I could not fathom that anything else could possibly go awry. I spent the duration of the trial on my aunt's couch yet again with only a smattering of clothes and incidentals. That couch crashing lasted close to a year as I hunted for a place to live that I could afford.

The witnesses on both sides of the fence, including our experts (who were held in the highest esteem in their respective fields), provided clear and precise testimony along with undeniable documented evidence. It all pointed to a slam dunk verdict in our favor. The jury returned with a stunning unanimous verdict… in favor of the poor doctor! Even after admitting under oath that her violation of every rule and law pertaining to her actions caused my mother's death, she still persuaded all 12 jurors that it wasn't her fault because she was bullied by her boss and the nurse practitioner.

The losing party at trial is responsible to pay attorney fees and costs to the opposing counsel. That tiny little invoice amounted to $150,000. The defendant made it clear there would be no negotiations for a reduction, PERIOD! Although the defendant was represented by her malpractice insurance company, and not one penny would come out of her pocket for her defense and there would be no benefit to her in any way by the insurance company negotiating their fees and costs, ultimately, she had the final word, and she was going for our jugulars. As the close of 2019 was fast approaching, our deadline to make good on this debt was coming due — in full.

I realize our settlement with the other defendants sounds like a tremendous amount of money, and it was. However, our attorney (worth every penny for his devotion, compassion, commitment, and love), received his 40% plus costs, which were exorbitant. And the remainder was split three ways between my sisters and me. My mother, like her mother, was as poor as a church mouse. This horrific lawsuit was the only legacy she would have for her daughters. Donna never had the opportunity to appreciate her blood money.

I remember when I first moved back to Los Angeles from Alaska, I heard Herbie Hancock give an experience about his Buddhist practice. He said that when he was a new practicing Buddhist, he had fallen quite ill and was hospitalized with no insurance and he ended up with overwhelming medical bills. He said that his prayer was that if he ever made it big in the music industry, the first thing he would do is repay everyone out of appreciation for saving his life. I never forgot that experience.

Interestingly, for the first several years after I moved back from Alaska in 2011, I was hospitalized many times and spent numerous nights in the ER with asthma. I couldn't breathe! I had no insurance, and I couldn't find a job for a full year. I was thousands of dollars in debt, all of which was eventually turned over to collection. I was also indebted to the tune of thousands of dollars to the IRS.

When my sisters and I received our settlements, my first order of business was to repay all my medical bills and clear the slate with the IRS forever. So, although my portion of settlement was substantial, my mom's gift enabled me to do just that… turn my life around. There are no words to express my deepest gratitude!

So, back to the impending close of 2019… knowing full well that every remaining penny I had to frugally secure a modest financial future for my senior years was about to be completely wiped out.

Daisaku Ikeda profoundly influenced my life many times over with this guidance: "When you clearly envision a victorious outcome, engrave it in your heart and are firmly convinced that you will attain it, your brain makes every effort to realize the mental image you have created. Then, through unceasing efforts, that victory is finally made reality. You are the playwright of your own victory."

With that in heart and mind, I chanted that the finality of this portion of my "play" would have an unimaginable ending. On New Year's Eve of 2019, my attorney called to say that the malpractice insurance adjuster contacted him to offer that even though they likely will be held liable for breaching their relationship with their client, they decided that my sisters and I had been through enough. They wrote off the full amount of our debt, and asked our attorney to relay to us from them, "Go have a good life!"

Sometimes what we envision as our victory might very well be something entirely unexpected.

22

GUARDIAN ANGELS

Back to the "why" of it all…

In the spring of 1998, after having purchased my very first computer, I discovered eBay and began exploring the myriad of possibilities in this marketplace. I have ALWAYS been one to plan well in advance. I even change lanes three miles ahead of my destination just in case someone decides to play road rage with me. Anyway, the holidays were only mere months away.

My young son was a Star Wars fanatic and my teenage daughter emerged into this world belting out Barbra Streisand tunes. Oh, man… what a treasure-trove of collectibles on eBay!

Delving into my fabulous new hobby, I found several Star Wars and Streisand collectibles. Then I wondered if there might be any Gogi Grant items up for bid. Lo and behold, I found all kinds of gems. How fun was this! Let the bidding begin! Much to my delight, everything I bid on (Star Wars, Streisand, Auntie Gogi), I WON!

For no apparent reason (although there's always a reason), I sent an email to one of the sellers of a Gogi item. This for no-apparent-reason email would end up being a life changing moment. Not one other seller received an email from me regarding my fabulous finds… only Charles Byrd in Hershey, PA. With heartfelt appreciation, I thanked him for this special gift… as my auntie's *Torch Time* album had disappeared long ago. In response, Mr. Byrd shared that he had been a big fan of hers, but because of his declining health, it was necessary for him to begin downsizing. He was elated that the album was going to me and asked how my aunt was doing. I told him she was well and still performing on occasion. He was thrilled to know that.

When he asked what I did for a living, I told him I was a "perspiring" writer, although my day job was supporting litigators in their high dramas. In response to that he said he had spent his life as a writer, editor, and publisher, then added he had an unusual specialty… paranormal psychology, ESP, psychic phenomenon, and synchronicity. He was finishing up his last project due to his health, when I quickly retorted, "I think you may have just one more little project." I told him about my compilation of amazing stories of synchronicity. He perked up and asked if I would consider allowing him to read them. Naturally, there could only be one answer to that, so off to the post office it went.

A couple of weeks later I received this letter from Charles along with an astounding writing he gifted me from his wife, Mary Nell.

Deborah -

Enclosed is the message received by Mary Nell. You should know that Mary Nell knew nothing about you when she did the reading, except that you are an email friend of mine who experiences "synchronicities" in her life; two of which I shared with our parapsychology group recently. I also gave her your birth name, adopted name, and present name. She did not know anything of your childhood experiences, your divorces, and did not see your book (Neither have I, but I will try to work on it this weekend). She has not seen any of your emails and I have not shared them with her, except for the two events I shared at our meeting. Thus, she spoke to the Guide with only minimum information.

Also, you should know that she is not a professional; receives messages for people only by special request and need; and has never received money or gifts for her assistance. She has spoken to spiritual beings as long as she can remember, but they first approached her in writing almost thirty years ago when she was beginning to write a note on a kitchen pad. Since that time she has received thousands of messages, but they are less frequent now because of the energy required. Through her, I also converse with the guides and have asked them hundreds of questions, talking with them about many subjects. The guides will appear any time Mary Nell requests, but they rarely interrupt her, except on occasion. In one instance, a few months ago, she was taking out the garbage of all things, and they spoke, giving her a message for a friend of ours who needed it badly. And just a few days ago, they gently interrupted her while she was writing a letter and gave her a message of importance. Thus, this communication has been a constant source of comfort and help to us throughout the years, and of immense purpose to others as well.

Concerning your writing: Mary Nell wrote this as she was receiving it from the messenger. It was written, as usual, almost faster than the mind can think, and occasionally words were missed and it is possible that she might have misinterpreted a word or two. She said it was one of the most intense writings she has ever done, and she had to stop twice to rest, which is most unusual for her. While the writing may seem short after being typewritten, (I keep all the originals) it was two and one quarter legal size pages written by hand. We did not understand it all, but this is not unusual. The Guides never say anything personal that will embarrass the recipient, and usually things that only the recipient will understand. Also, the reading may have to be read many times for a full understanding, and sometimes there are things in the writings which you may not understand today, but may be clearer days, weeks, or even months from now. Nevertheless, we hope it is helpful to you.

We will be thinking of your sister and pray she recovers quickly. I also have a sister who is quite ill; a mother who is slowly dying in Nashville; an uncle who helped raise me who is in critical condition in Kentucky; and a brother-in-law who is seriously ill; thus we have been quite concerned lately and I have gotten a little behind in my work and my editing. Take care and I'll look forward to hearing from you again.

Writing for Deborah Ann Favorite
By Mary Nell Byrd
Received July 22, 1999

This one - this one whose intensity of thought goes far beyond the norm is a product of endless time - a product by which much has been accessed and processed through the eons of time and into the present, although it is endless.

Though we must embark upon on a time period which will be most difficult - Let us start from a point of interest when this was first realized - At a moment of time in early childhood when feelings would enhance the thought, not understanding and with nowhere to turn - this feeling of awe was overwhelming her - so it would go hidden but into the resources of her subconscious. These thoughts dwelled there and were never understood. In time these thoughts began to surface in various ways - many times the thoughts were not good - brought forth by not understanding, so still they dwelled unfulfilled in the resources of the mind.

So this went forth to many areas of existences bringing many entities of souls gathering to try to get the messages across - thus more confusing, and this went on and on and on. We could carry this forth to the present with details, but this was the beginning and now we need to dwell on this period of time. This one understands now the past - but what to do with the present is what is the prime focus now.

We are here to help - to explain and to try to sort out all of this to the advantage of the many entities which have been a part and who are a part of the soul, portions which become <u>whole.</u> (*This emphasis was that of the Guide - not Mary Nell)*

To understand is to bear the fruit of the time - To be used in such a capacity is to acknowledge the unique soul of this entity. Far and beyond time this one has evolved - even before the beginning. We have come to a time in history when knowledge is coming

forth from all directions and the complexity of it all can bother the searches of thinking because the human mind cannot understand or even try to comprehend the true meaning - Not now, not until the completion of the earthly existence, and perhaps not even then.

But the message here is this. There are those who are sent from far reaches of the universe for purposes never totally understood, but meanings are clear to the sender, for the mission is to touch entities who are untouchable and to understand the un-understandable and to love the unlovable and to bring peace to the ones who have no peace and on and on and on...... This brings forth unions of individual existences and creates moments to enhance souls in a ------------(*These words were lost in the communication, thus the Guide continued below....*)

We must say this again - this creates moments to enhance the meaning of what all of this creates. The sender is the creator, in sorts, and the message is to continue the search for all who need this touch.

Now as to earthly matters of personal note - To achieve all this sometimes causes personal situations more pain in the physical world - but the soul and its entity is growing in bonds of eternity.

What do we say to those who say, Why?

We say nothing and go on and pursue all that is paramount in one's life.

Now you are the one to whom all this has been acknowledged and achieved. Your gifts of many are from the beginning when all this knowledge first penetrated the child mind to try to understand - until a time when it could all surface and begin the journey to understanding. Your life is a journey of complexities but filled with the awe of love and peace internally. Focus now on <u>You</u>, the inner <u>You</u> who needs refreshment of energy for your continuing journey - for it has only begun.

There is a great joy, peace, and happiness ahead for you. It is already there and will continue to enhance your life and those around you.

Continue your path to fulfillment and peace--------

Before receiving this gift, Charles called me on the phone. He encouraged me to get my editing done and have my work published as soon as possible. He felt my experiences were not only unique and powerful, but timely. He asked my permission to share some of my stories at one of his paranormal, ESP, synchronistic, psychic gatherings. I was honored and, of course I said, "Yes, please!" Enclosed with these letters and a photo of Charles and Mary Nell, were two of his own books, *To Fly with the Angels* and *Cry for Marsella*. As life would have it, our encounter was brief, but certainly not without profundity.

In 2003, I received an email from Mary Nell telling me that on October 21, Charles passed away. She wanted me to know because she said he held a special place in his heart for me. Only recently I discovered that Mary Nell joined him on March 25, 2019. I will never forget either of these two magnificent humans.

^^^

The Buddhist organization, SGI-USA, was holding a conference at our Florida Nature & Culture Center in Weston, Florida, the weekend of March 9, 2018 — nearly 20 years after my encounter with Charles and Mary Nell.

I arrived at the airport with ample time on my hands and plugged my flight information into the machine for my boarding pass — multiple times, and in multiple machines — to no avail. I ended up in the line I didn't want to stand in, and once I reached the clerk, she promptly printed out my pass. No problemo.

After a long wait at the gate, the plane finally began boarding. Just when it was my turn to scan my pass and board, I was summoned to the desk.

The clerk asked to see my ticket. After examining it and comparing it to her computer screen, she told me I was not booked on that flight. After a bit of back and forth with, "Yes I am!" "No, you're not!", her superior asked to see my pass. Apologizing for the misunderstanding, she explained that the other woman wasn't aware that my seat assignment had been changed at the last minute. She graciously printed out a corrected pass and I boarded the plane.

NOTE NO. 1: *I was now assigned to a seat that I was not supposed to be in.*

Personally, I like being on the isle just in case I need to stroll to the Little Gargoyle's room. In the shuffling of the seating, I ended up at the window. A lovely Australian couple joined me taking the middle and aisle seats. They were about my age-ish. Gordon told me he was a pilot for Qantas and that he and his wife were on holiday heading for Jamaica. Originally, their seat assignments were in separate rows, and they had requested, if possible, to be seated together.

NOTE NO. 2: *Their seats were both reassigned and now they, too, were in seats they were not supposed to be in.*

To make things easier for me to recall, they introduced themselves as Ruth and Gordon. My only challenge would be remembering either *Harold and Maude*, or *Rosemary's Baby*. I can do that.

Right after takeoff, Gordon got up to make his way to the loo. Ruth turned to me and quietly inquired, "Are you a writer?" Catching me a bit off guard, I replied, "Well… I guess I'm kind of a 'perspiring' writer." Nodding she continued, "I'm so sorry for intruding. I don't ordinarily approach people like this, and I don't generally announce to a total stranger that I'm a psychic, but I'm receiving a very powerful message right now."

As I examined her, I came to the immediate conclusion that she didn't look like a psychic. She was quite conservatively dressed in a lovely silk blouse, wool blazer, and slacks. Her hair was blond and tastefully styled at shoulder length, and she wore just enough makeup to enhance her natural beauty. I would have taken her for a successful businesswoman or a high-end realtor. But what do I know from psychics?

When she saw my curiosity, she continued. "I'm sensing the presence of a man. Kind face. Tall. Older gentleman. He is with a woman who has soft brown shoulder-length hair. They both exude kindness and warmth. He is telling me something about four sections. I don't know what that means. And there is something about the number 20. I don't understand if 20 has anything to do with how many pieces in a section. But I believe it is about your writing. Oh, he says you will complete it in the year 2020. He also says that when you're ready, he will guide you for publishing. They have been watching over you for a very long time."

Charles and Mary Nell Byrd

Although I have never sought guidance from a psychic, I did have my cards read once at a health fair. To be perfectly honest, it too was quite an extraordinary reading.

Mystified by her description, I remarked that I thought I knew who she was talking about. I went on to share my eBay story with her, and the picture of Charles and Mary Nell that he sent to me. Her eyes widened in astonishment when I mentioned Charles Byrd. "You knew Charles Byrd?!" When I explained that I knew him only briefly, she told me they knew each other through his organization of psychics and channelers.

We both took a deep breath as every hair on my arms stood at attention. She went on to tell me other things. Specific things regarding my mom, my grandmother and my sister, Nancy.

She sensed something that had to do with rings… many rings. They each had a story, she said. "One of the rings has a large green stone the color of your mom's eyes." Before my mom passed away, she gifted me a gorgeous green tourmaline ring. She said she wanted me to have it because it was the only thing she had of value.

My sister, Nancy, adored rings, and she bejeweled every finger, including her thumbs, with them. When Nancy passed away, my sisters and I divvied up her ring collection so we each would have a special part of her. I managed to abscond with the ones I loved most.

When Grandmom was dying of cancer, she summoned each of us to come visit. She had always been as poor as a church mouse… odd comparison for a nice Jewish girl. She was lying comfortably in her bed when I arrived. She had an eight-inch square department store gift box sitting next to her. This was where she stored her bootie… costume jewelry. I sat on the bed beside her. She handed me the box and told me I could pick one item to remember her by. I reached into the box and found another tiny gift box, like one from a jewelry counter that might contain a delicate bracelet. As I lifted it out of the bigger box, my fingers fumbled, and it fell open onto her chest. Resting underneath the thin layer of cotton was a tiny circle and a silver locket. Grandmom's reaction was one of absolute surprise. "Where did you find that?!" I told her it fell out of the little box. Tears of delight welled up in her eyes as she declared I was the winner of the BIG prize. Then she shared her story:

"When Grandpop and I got married, I was 15. We had to elope because our parents would never have approved of our marriage. Grandpop's family thought they were aristocrats, and my family were paupers. I had to borrow $5 for a marriage license, a dress and shoes, and a ring. This was my first wedding ring. I thought I had lost it years ago. My brother made this locket and gifted it to me for our wedding." Yes, I certainly won the prize… the most personal items in her little box of life's treasures.

Two decades prior to my trip to Florida, I had organized my stories, essays, and poetry into the four seasons of life: Spring, Summer, Fall and Winter. In my quirkiest fashion, I drew the four life seasons from my perspective on yellow Post-Its: (1) a little girl's dangling feet bearing lacy socks and buckle shoes; (2) sassy high heeled shoes on a young lady; (3) comfortable shoes on a middle-aged woman; and (4) granny shoes on an elderly senior — all viewed from under the door of a public restroom stall.

The idea of completing my manuscript of phenomenal synchronicities in the year 2020 remained at the forefront of my mind. Even so, I made no real effort to do anything about it.

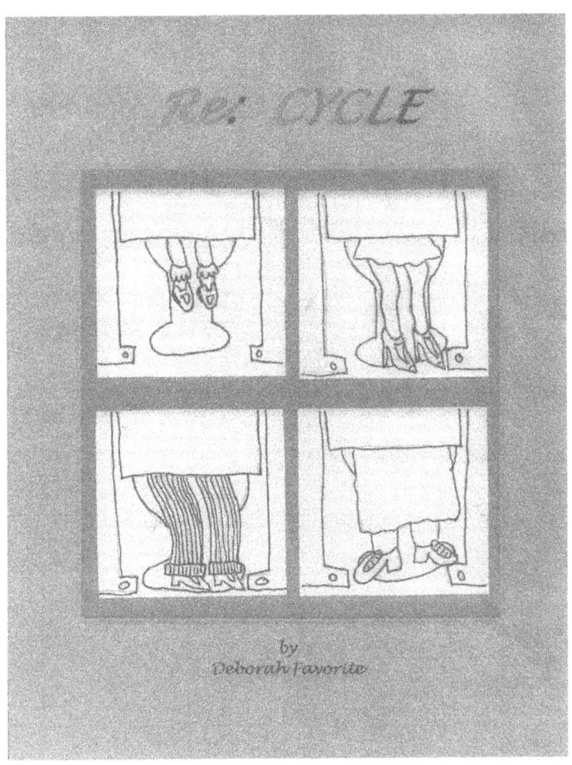

2020 New Year's Resolution! COMPLETE YOUR BOOK! Charles and Mary Nell are watching you and they're getting bored!

I dug through my bins of photos until I found the one of Charles and Mary Nell Byrd. I stuck it in my notebook so it would be where it was supposed to be when I needed it. I pulled out my notebook and began reading my drafts. But instead of editing all those amazing magical events, I distracted myself and began beating down the brambles and tall weeds attempting to carve out my autobiography.

What a struggle! It was emotionally packed, filled with pain and disappointments. I was overwhelmed by my COVID isolation and simply did not want my journey to continue. I was venting all the unhappiness I could muster as our New Year of Pandemic marched on. All I could think about were the heartbreaking events of my life. And now this was how it would all end. It was magnified by the daily disintegration of our world, the oppressive 120-degree heat in Palm Springs where I live, and the raging fires up and down the western states, particularly California and my backyard. I was depressed and couldn't stop crying. I felt hopeless.

One day in early August of 2020, I received a book in the mail from my cousin Diane… the one who introduced me to the Buddhism of Nam myoho renge kyo in 1974. The book was titled *Big Magic — Creative Living Without Fear*, by Elizabeth Gilbert.

Not wanting to acquiesce to someone wagging their well-intentioned finger in my face, the book remained on my coffee table for a couple of weeks. I'd glance at the cover now and again as I continued sliding down my dark rabbit hole. We are in the midst of a global pandemic, and I can wallow in my self-pity if I want to!

Like any good activist, I spend an inordinate amount of time absorbing the news of the day. I do a lot of activating on social media. After all, isn't it my duty to ensure that the world knows just how bad it all is? If I don't do it, then who will? As the months of 2020 pressed on, I noticed that most of the posts on Facebook from my 5000 friends, rapidly morphed into despair, sadness, hopelessness, disease, anger, death, hunger, violence. These were not news articles; they were personal postings of fellow humans. With all the dark challenges we've experienced in our history, I don't think there has been anything quite like the evil rhetoric and divisiveness of today. The energy can only be compared to blood sucking vampires. My chanting was even pathetic. It was incredibly difficult to maintain any sense of hope or positivity. Now and again, I would make myself shut it off and allow the healing medicine of music to fill my pores. That always works… temporarily.

I began noticing all the angry and crying emojis in response to my news postings. In my desire to make sure the world remained informed, I realized that I was perpetuating every ounce of darkness I was feeling. Misery loves company, right?

As the close of August neared, I poked my nose inside the cover of *Big Magic* and from the first sentence I was hooked. A quarter of the way in, I was beginning to feel like a wilted flower that had been doused with rain. My chanting became more focused, my head was clearing its cobwebs, and I renewed my determination to finish my book… the one that I dearly hoped would inspire others to climb out of their suffering, especially with all that's going on around us.

Early in September, I was on Facebook when a pop-up ad soliciting a numerology reading appeared. Hey, why not! It was 42 pages long! I didn't feel like investing that much time reading it, so I saved it on my computer for another day.

On September 17, I pulled the photo of Charles and Mary Nell from my notebook and placed it on my keyboard, leaning it against my computer screen so I could have them near me… perhaps to act as my muse.

Before opening the computer folder where I stored my writing, I decided to read the numerology report. Maybe it would inspire something in me to wake up. I read it slowly, savoring every word. It was chock full of gems. It described me to a tee… good, bad, and indifferent. I glanced at my buddies sitting on my keyboard and said, "Okay, let's get started!"

I have dozens and dozens of folders, and dozens of folders in the folders, on my computer. The folder where I saved the numerology report is titled SPIRITUAL. I had been saving things in that folder for years. Aside from saving things for some future enlightenment, I'm not sure that I have ever actually opened that folder… not until the 17th of September, in the Year of Perfect Vision — 2020. As I was about to hit save to preserve my report for posterity, I noticed one of the many folders was marked Charles Byrd. I assumed its content would be his letter to me, along with Mary Nell's channeling message. I clicked it open. Before my eyes were 39 emails that I had received from Charles ranging in time from 1998 through 2003. I was stunned! I looked at their photo and then spent the next few hours reading them… digesting them… pondering them. As much as I thought I remembered about our relationship, I had no recollection of it spanning over so many years. As I absorbed each one, I was able to pull out vague remembrances of having read them before. I was amazed at their depth of intimacy and friendship. I wondered if I would ever have discovered those treasured letters had I not ordered that numerology report (the one whose ad popped up on my Facebook page uninvited). The psychic on the flight to Florida said he would lead me.

I decided to do a quick perusal of Facebook before I dug in. The moment I opened my page, another ad popped up from Steve Harrison (Harrison is my son's middle name). It was an infomercial. Steve wanted to know if I was looking to publish a book. He wanted to know if, in my desire to write one, I had ever felt like, "Who would want to hear what I have to say?" or "I have no credentials." Yada, yada, yada! It sounded like he was talking to me. He went on to say that his job is to help nonfiction writers complete their work and get published. "Do you have a message of inspiration? Are your experiences meaningful, heartfelt, and encouraging? Do you have a passion for your experiences? Will they move people's hearts? Well, if you do, I will teach you how to lay out your book and prepare the blueprint for writing, and then I will guide you to publish." I promptly ordered Mr. Harrison's workshop. I realized that the grueling story I had been attempting to write was NOT what I had sent to Charles in 1998. What Charles had encouraged me to finish and get published, and then on the plane made a special appearance from high above the clouds, were my stories of synchronicity, and he promised he would guide me to get it published... okay... it might be a stretch, but it sure didn't feel like a stretch.

I put my notebook aside and opened a new one. Then I opened a bound copy of my draft stories, the ones I had sent to Charles two decades before. Flipping through the pages, I was amazed at how many of these magnificent episodes had slipped my memory.

I thought that might be a prudent time for me to investigate Steve Harrison's program on the fastest and most efficient way to get my book written. Embarking upon my educational opportunity, I found myself glued to his every word. Piecing together all the ins and outs of successfully organizing things really began to flow.

I had been editing from a bound draft I had and found it to be too cumbersome. I remembered that in 1998 I had a few copies bound. I grabbed my step stool and climbed into my hall closet where I knew old files were stored on the top shelf. In one of the expandable folders, I could see the tops of three bound books that I was sure were the extra copies. I struggled to release one of them when a paperclipped document sprung out and fell to the ground. When I finally released the book from the expandable folder, I stepped down and picked up the papers that had scattered all over the floor to discover they were six pages of typed edit suggestions from Charles that were dated August 9, 1999. I had no recollection of them, I barely remembered the 39 emails I found on my computer, many of them commenting on my stories and encouraging me to get them in final form and publish! In addition, the copy of the bound draft I pulled out of the file happened to be the one I had sent to Charles that displayed his handwritten comments.

There is no question in my mind that Charles and Mary Nell are embarking upon this wonderful adventure with me. Their presence is potent and ripe with animated delight!

∧ ∧ ∧

On August 13, 1998, I took my son on a field trip to Los Angeles. On the way home, we were driving down Melrose Avenue when I noticed the Bodhi Tree Bookstore. I had wanted to go in there for years but never had. I found a place to park across the street and we headed into the store. What a gold mine!

We browsed for quite a while gathering armfuls of inspiration. We checked out at the register and just as we approached the car, I said to my son, "I'll be right back, I forgot something." I rushed back in to see if there was such a thing as a calendar of events. I didn't know if they had events, but there it was… a stack of flyers on the front counter. I grabbed one and left.

I had just finished reading *The Celestine Prophecy* and had become a major fan. I had not yet read *The Celestine Vision* or *The Celestine Prophecy: An Experiential Guide*. As I jumped in the driver's seat, I glanced at the flyer that screamed out in glaring print that Carol Adrienne, the co-author of *The Celestine Prophecy: An Experiential Guide* was going to be at the Bodhi Tree for a lecture and book signing for her new book, *The Purpose of Your Life*.

So, on August 13, 1998, I headed out to the Bodhi Tree for my second excursion.

The lecture area was a small intimate parlor-like room. There were only about 10 people in attendance. Her lecture was fascinating and for a good deal of it her eyes pierced mine. It felt like she was either putting me under a spotlight or trying to read me.

After the lecture, I waited until the other nine people had gone before I went up to the table to have her sign my book. Her eye-piercing reignited when she said to me, "You are incredibly psychic!" I modestly looked around to be sure she was addressing me. "Well, I don't really think I'm psychic, but I do have this thing where I seem to be more like a gatherer. I don't necessarily think I know when things are going to happen, but I have amazing experiences of unbelievable coincidences." I told her they are so extraordinary and I'm not sure how to deliberately make them happen. But I told her I believe they happen for some purpose but I'm not sure what I'm supposed to do with it. She signed my book, handed it to me and said, "You're supposed to write about them."

While experiencing this wonderful relationship with Charles and Mary Nell from the otherworld, on the morning of October 6, 2020, while I was doing my morning chanting, I looked at Carol's book that I had taken out of my library to have at the ready. Ready for what? I'm not sure, but I placed my hand on the cover and said to the universe, "Something needs to happen with this today!" I had recently told my Auntie Toni that I wanted to find a way to locate her because I'd like to ask if she might endorse my book.

I opened her book while I was still chanting to see if there might be any interesting acknowledgments in the back. Tucked between the back cover and the jacket were some folded papers. I pulled them out to find the calendar of events for Carol's appearances back in 1998, which included a flyer about the content of her book… in front of my eyes, on the flyer, was her phone number, fax, and email address.

THE
PRESENT

Riches, prestige, everything can be lost. But the happiness in your heart can only be dimmed; it will always be there, as long as you live, to make you happy again.

———————

Anne Frank

FALLING IN LOVE... WITH ME

I remember when *A Chorus Line* came out ...it was 1976 and I was 27... my mom was 46. Because it was so new to the world, it had not yet become kitchen table talk, and neither had the music.

One evening my parents were out to dinner at a famous steakhouse in Santa Monica. While waiting for a table, they took a seat at the piano bar to enjoy a cocktail. My mom asked the piano player if he knew *What I Did for Love*, and he indignantly retorted, "No, lady, and I really don't care!"

Well, I resemble those comments. I certainly don't wear them as a badge of honor, but karmically speaking, I suppose I spent a great deal of my life looking for love in all the wrong places. The places were not actually the issue, it was who was present during the search... and that would be me. Although the places changed, the essence of the criteria of the search never did... only the landscape. The main point was finding someone who would fall head over heels in love with me, because one thing was for certain... I was not going to do it!

So, between hating my parents for all the things they didn't do right and hating myself because of all the things they didn't do right, I assumed there must be someone out there someplace who would be more than happy to take on that responsibility. I have had five failed marriages, and without a calculator I can't count the number of just as bad, if not worse, relationships in between. Every time a notch was added to the headboard, my self-loathing increased tenfold. My anger and disappointment that none of those guys came close to bestowing on me the love I didn't deserve, it would take most of my adult life to realize my part in all of that. I could rake them in alright, but it never dawned on me that there might be a thread that linked the failures together. The reasonable conclusion could only be that men are jerks, and that obviously is NOT my fault!

The truth of the matter is that it wasn't only men that I was involved with who were jerks… it was my mother, my fathers, my bosses, my former friends, my neighbors… they were all jerks… eventually!

I went up and down the weight scale just about as often as I changed men. Then, in the year 2000, one of my coworkers told me about a surgery that Carnie Wilson had to lose weight. Wow, that seemed pretty, drastic! Then, she told me she seriously wanted to do the same. I began to research that procedure and in fairly, short order, she and another co-worker and myself decided to consult with a surgeon.

The vote was unanimous… we were going for it! All for one and one for all!

My friends' reasoning to move forward with this radical procedure had to do with their health issues, whereas mine predominantly revolved around fat being a grand hiding place and I was ready to step out from behind it. My psychology was flawed though because I had been in a relationship with someone for three years while I was fat. The day after we came home from a romantic getaway for Valentine's Day, he dumped me. He never told me he was dumping me… he simply disappeared… no explanation… no Dear Jane letter… nothing… nada.

So, the idea of permanently stepping into gorgeousness would unquestionably guarantee someone… anyone… coming to my rescue!

Within what seemed minutes, I shed 100 pounds… I was stunning! Then came the tummy tuck! Then came the dating site profiles. Then came the overwhelming messages of undying love for me… sight unseen… well, not entirely… they could definitely see me… my photos were right there.

My dance card was spilling out all over the floor… one jerk after another. Some simply were just not a fit, but however you looked at it, I never stopped trying to squeeze my big foot into that tiny glass slipper.

One day, I received a message from Michael who lived in Anchorage, Alaska. Although my profile clearly stated I wasn't interested in meeting anyone who lived more than 10 miles away (I was in the Los Angeles area), I caved and met men who lived in Orange County, Long Beach, the Inland Empire; one man flew out from Minnesota, so we met in Las Vegas. That was interesting. Hell, I was willing to fall in love with anyone, anywhere, any time. But my beautiful, and sexy self, did not appear to be attracting anyone who might be looking for the same outcome… not with me anyway.

So, when Michael in Alaska continued a pen pal courtship and then moved on to hours on the telephone, my fairytale seemed to be coming to light. After a few months of this romance, I hopped on a plane for the Fourth of July holiday and headed for Anchorage. Michael and I were the same age, 54. He was having a midlife career change and was in nursing school. He also played bass in a rock band. We had an amazing three days together — I met his family and friends, hung out at the bar where his band was playing, and toured around a small part of Alaska. A great time was had by all.

We continued with our daily phone calling and then he said he wanted me to move to Alaska. That was something I hadn't really thought much about. What I mostly thought about was how perfect our little fairytale romance was… why ruin it? I no longer had my fat suit to hide behind, but 3500 miles came in as a secure second.

We talked about it every day for a few months. I stressed over everything I would be giving up if I decided to make that decision. I owned my own home. I had been at my job with a terrific law firm with mega-benefits for 10 years, my family and friends and Buddhist community were all there, although I did have extreme problems with my son and my mother. My daughter had moved to San Francisco a couple of years before, and I was still spending between three and four hours a day commuting back and forth to work. I had no real life, and it felt like I had no real reason to stay. But Michael needed to convince me that this was really it for him. So, he showered me with poetry, sent me cards, letters, and flowers.

In early fall, I put my home on the market and it sold in a matter of days. I had only been in that house for a year and a half and made $180,000 profit on it. I believe it was the day after I closed escrow and held that nice little check in my hand that the real estate market crashed. I thought it was a blaring neon sign that I had made the right decision. I sold just about everything I owned, and Michael flew down (at my expense) to meet my family and friends, shipped off everything I intended on keeping, said my tearful goodbyes and off we went into the sunset in my sleek and sexy, slate-colored Mitsubishi Eclipse.

Michael planned the detailed itinerary. The fairytale honeymoon road trip (we weren't married) would take 10 days from beginning to end (at my expense). From sunup on the third day until we crossed the finish line and into infinity, Michael did not speak one word to me. At some point during that third day, all I could do was kick myself and silently scream, "WHAT HAVE YOU DONE?!"

The day we arrived in Anchorage I awoke in the middle of the night to find him sitting at his computer flirting with someone on a dating site.

Bright and early the next morning, I made a call to the president of the Anchorage Bar Association who was a longtime friend of one of the partners in the Los Angeles firm where I had worked. He was privy to everything that went on in all the law offices in Anchorage, and he had been expecting my call. It just so happened that he knew of an opening for a legal secretary in one of the downtown firms. He said that if his Los Angeles buddy raved about me, he would highly recommend me for the position. I was hired on the spot and started my new job the following Monday.

Before I began my new job, I found a lovely, brand-new townhouse that had just fallen out of escrow and because of the sizable down payment I was offering, I was able to close escrow in two weeks. That was the duration of my couch sleeping ordeal at Michael's.

I was about to embark upon a new life chapter filled with wonder, joy, devastation, and self-discovery. Thank you, Michael, for being the impetus that got me there. Your mission, as it turns out, was a great one!

^ ^ ^

After my interview, I drove around downtown to do some sightseeing. A few blocks from my new office, I spied a quaint little street and turned to do some exploring. On the second lot from the corner sat an adorable log cabin with a split-rail fence surrounding it. Two large trees shaded either side of the front yard. It was early fall, and there had already been a light dusting of snow that blanketed the grass and trees. Miniature white lights along the roofline, the large picture window, and strewn amongst the tree branches, cast their sparkle on the snow while smoke danced around the chimney. If I wasn't already in escrow, this enticing winter wonderland would have had my name written all over it.

Launching my new adventure, I moved into my beautiful new home. It was located about three miles from downtown and sat at the base of the Chugach Mountains. My newest thrill was having moose grazing in my yard, oftentimes with a baby in tow. They don't get snow days off in Anchorage, but a moose in your driveway warrants a free pass for being late to work. One day as I was pulling into the grocery store parking lot, a black bear darted across and into the alleyway, most likely to dig through the dumpster searching for supper.

My new co-workers were a pretty friendly bunch, and my social life began to blossom. I found a weekly dance place that I began to frequent, and one of the attorneys I worked with took me under his wing and introduced me to some of the local theater players.

My dating continued and much to my dismay, they didn't seem to be much different in Alaska than they were in Los Angeles. Eventually, I met someone who wooed me with cards and letters and flowers, and he was a mighty fine dancer. He wasn't really my type, but I was 55, and that glass slipper was looking mighty fine, even if it was a size 6, and I still donned an 8 ½.

Eventually I danced into my fifth marriage, but not before I was persuaded by him to buy a big fixer-upper and rent my townhouse to his son and daughter-in-law. I had the money, and he had the brawn, and then I had the brawn. We demolished the inside of the house and did a remarkable remodeling (at my expense). Then, three years and another divorce older, life became a living hell. I needed to find a place to live because he refused to leave. I toured some rentals for a couple of weeks… none of which I would want to live in. One early morning, I opened my computer to browse the ads. First one up was for a charming log cabin downtown with a phone number and an address listed. There was no way to know if that was my log cabin unless I drove over there to check it out. Before making a beeline downtown, I left a message that I was interested in renting and then my sidekick, Luna, my Springer Spaniel, and I barreled into the car. Wowie Zowie! It was my cabin! We raced back home, and I jumped back on the computer. The ad WAS GONE!!! My home phone did NOT have a caller ID, so the phone number disappeared into the ethernet.

I started chanting feverishly… you simply cannot have a dangling carrot like that and not take it seriously… you simply cannot!

The next afternoon a man called to say he was following up on my interest in the log cabin. Within five minutes of posting the ad, he had 50 calls, so he took it down. I told him about the first time I happened upon it five years before when I had first moved to Anchorage. I told him I was convinced that this was not a coincidence… it was a meant to be! I asked if I could see it that afternoon and he told me there was a tenant living there. I explained that I was going through a divorce, and I had to move by the first of August (it was the second week in July), my son was expecting my first grandchild on July 22, and I had planned to be in California for the birth, and I had to secure something before I left. He seemed to think it would be okay if I saw it and gave me the phone number of the tenant. I called the number, but the voice message sounded like a recording for an aerospace company. I left a message anyway but hadn't gotten a call back by the time I was leaving work. My co-worker insisted we drive over and knock on the door. I didn't think it was a good idea to barge in like that, but we went anyway. Instead of knocking, I decided to stick a note on the front door. The tenant saw me through the window and greeted me as I was heading up the walkway. He assumed I was the one who called, and he invited us in. It was a filthy mess, but my name was indeed written all over it.

I called the owner to see if he'd been in there lately. He said no, and so I proposed (knowing there were 49 other people who wanted it, most likely without demands) that in exchange for me doing the cleanup, painting and carpet shampooing, he would waive the security deposit and the last month's rent. I knew if I were the landlord, I would be hesitant to allow a tenant to douse a brush in a bucket of paint on my property, so I told him about my house and the work I (we) did and offered for him to come and see it, and then make a decision. He agreed and when he saw how gorgeous the house was, we signed the lease then and there and I gave him a check.

Luna and I loved that little log cabin, as did all my friends and fellow Buddha Buddies. We built so many wonderful memories living there. But, the truth of the matter was, I was still on the path of following the dangling carrot of benefits without looking in the real mirror of my life.

My husband took me to the cleaners in the divorce. He owed me $100,000. Without my knowledge, he let the house go into foreclosure after saying he would buy me out. The down payment, the out-of-pocket funds, and the enormous credit card debt to remodel, plus debt to the IRS (which was supposed to be 'joint') all fell on me. Because the mortgage loan was connected to my accounts, Wells Fargo swept them clean with no due process, for his intentional discontinuation of payment. After a fierce court battle, he ended up only having to paying me $10,000, and for that I had to hire an investigator to find him and attach his salary. Then I ended up having two emergency back surgeries within a few days of each other (secondary to remodeling the house), and then I was fired from my job for missing a period at the end of a sentence. I looked at the office manager and said, "Wow, I'm 61 years old… I can't believe I just missed a period." Having no inkling of the humor in that statement, she uncaringly escorted me to the elevator. My son had not spoken to me in nearly a decade, and he made it clear that he did not want me in his or his kids' lives. And, my mother and I had never resolved our issues from my lifetime of blame.

For the first time in decades of practice and tremendous carrot-dangling benefits, I found myself in front of my Buddhist altar sobbing in total defeat.

The first conversation I had with myself went something like this:

"Do you have a roof over your head?" "YES."

"Do you have food in the refrigerator?" "YES."

"Do you have ANYONE in your life who loves you?" "YES."

"Are there Nazis kicking your door down?" "NO."

"Then what are you crying about?!"

I sat in front of my altar chanting until my life condition was elevated… until I was brave enough to look at myself… until I found the courage to acknowledge my own dignity… and until I pulled out the wisdom to know how to move forward. Then my decision was made. It was time to go home… to Los Angeles. It was time to face the real music. It was time to take the bull by the horns, no matter how long it might take and transform my relationships with my son, my mother… and myself. It sounded absolutely terrifying! But I knew in the depths of my being it was time! The truth of the matter was that the challenge could not possibly be any more painful than the reality I was already living in, right?

I sold just about everything I owned, called my Auntie Toni to ask if Luna and I could stay with her just until I landed a job. Being that I nearly always landed a job at my first interview (I mean I had glowing references from some of the most prestigious law firms in the country), I knew it would be for only a short time. She reluctantly said "yes."

I shipped some things off to Los Angeles, and then Luna and I headed down the Al-Can Highway. It took about 12 days to get back to Los Angeles. Once I got over my fear of traveling alone, the trip was magnificent.

As it turned out, I could not find a job to save my life for nearly a year. I chanted two to three hours a day, sometimes more, and I spent six to eight hours a day searching, circulating my resume, modifying my resume to fit certain kinds of job descriptions. I registered with a nanny service. I circulated flyers for services to organize homes or offices, cooking for the elderly and driving them to appointments, picking up kids after school and helping with homework and transporting them to sports practices. I was registered with every headhunter in Los Angeles. I could not even land an interview.

FINALLY, an old co-worker referred me to an attorney who was opening his own firm with two other attorneys. Oddly, one of them was the sister of Trish, the attorney I worked for in Beverly Hills in 1985. They hired me on the spot.

FINALLY, Luna and I were able to move into our own little studio apartment right down the street from Toni in West Los Angeles. BTW, that year-long stay was one of the highlights of my life… Toni and I developed a bond of friendship like no other I've ever had. I am profoundly grateful every day for her.

My mom had been living with my sister Donna for several years and I began spending time with her… intimate time with her. We covered a lot of territory in our conversations. I learned a great deal about her personal struggles and challenges since the time of the accident in 1956. She had a lot to share. I had a lot to learn. The more I chanted to absorb, the deeper my compassion grew. She apologized profusely for all the pain she caused me by never stepping in to protect me from my dad's abuse. We spent a lot of time laughing and crying and our metamorphosis became grand!

In the meantime, my son continued with his decision to keep me out of his life. He had been rejecting me since he was in the 6th grade, and it only compounded over time. He was married and had three young children. My deepest prayer was to have an opportunity to change the horrible poison I had with him. I never understood where it came from, but he was obviously suffering, as was I.

So long as my incredible synchronicities kept unfolding, I could keep on track and continue looking in the mirror at myself, no matter how difficult and painful it all was.

A few years after returning to Los Angeles, my son called me. He said he was in the area and wanted to know if we could meet for dinner. And so, we did. After some uncomfortable small talk, he told me he was separated from his wife, he had lost his job and he had nowhere to go. Sounded like a familiar tale. I welcomed him to stay with me in my 300 square foot studio apartment… the one where Luna and I barely had room to turn around in. And so, he did. He was deeply distraught, and I worried every day about him. Some days I feared going home because I wasn't sure what I might find. He had always been a brilliant writer, and he began to pour his attention into storytelling. He completed a few screenplays and the first book in a fantasy trilogy. Each one so vividly creative!

After some time, he shared with me what had happened to him to cause his lashing out at me. I was stunned! Since childhood he had been harboring an unimaginable wound… someone told him that I had never wanted him, that I was sorry he was born. My heart shattered into a million pieces that he had suffered for so many years over something so malicious and false… but, my prayer had been answered! The universe provided the opportunity to profoundly transform our relationship. And so, it did. Naturally, it took time. It took time for me to find compassion for the person who filled my son with such venom. It took time for me to take responsibility to not perpetuate any further hurt or harm.

Over the years, my son and I have developed an abundance of respect, compassion, love, and friendship that continues to blossom in deep joy and happiness. I have a fabulous relationship with my three amazing grandkids. And I am so grateful for the ever-present evolution in my life. And to be perfectly honest, I wouldn't change a thing. It has all brought richness and profound meaning to my purpose.

Of course, my daughter and I have had our moments (she was a teenager once), but my challenge regarding her life primarily spun around the deep pain I experienced with her father — his increasing contempt for me in our marriage, and then the betrayal — his infidelity with my good friend and confidant, her blatant nastiness toward me after they married and her disrespect for my daughter. Breaking through those chains ultimately fulfilled my resolve for my daughter to have a wonderful relationship with her dad. And through it all, he and I have become very special friends developing a unique alternative family.

Some folks come into Buddhist practice knowing the moment they walk through the door that this is what they've been seeking all along. It simply feels natural. Some take it on gradually and grow into their shoes at a slow or moderate pace. For me, because of the gravity of my darkness, it took a long time to unearth the candle buried in my cave and strike that flint. But the glow of one candle will light up a cave that has been immersed in darkness for thousands of years. So, the extraordinary experiences I have been so fortunate to have lived were essential to keep me going. Without them I would not have been able to find the true purpose of my life. That purpose is not all the magical benefits… the perfect job, the perfect home, the perfect new love, the perfect parking space. They're a nice icing on the cake, but those things all exist outside of myself, but they were the impetus to uncover and bring forth my courageous self to fight and conquer my own fundamental darkness.

My personal experiences all revolved around relationships… relationships with parents, children, spouses, employers, neighbors, friends, horn honkers and, most importantly… the one I now have with myself.

I spent most of my life seeking out someone… anyone… to take on the responsibility to love me, but they were all doomed to fail miserably, because the reality is, that's my job. So, with each failure, I'd pack it up and move to another location, always looking for a fresh start. The problem was that every time I packed it up for a new beginning, I was always there when I arrived.

Coming to the place where I lost everything, even after years and years of practice, ended up being the most valuable and profoundly significant turning point… the great challenge of transforming from the inside and creating the real benefit of falling in love with me.

The practice of this Buddhism does not magically make our lives problem free. We don't suddenly live in La-La-Land. We get to continue living as who we are with our myriad of faults in tow. We do, however, receive a mirror like no other to reflect on our imperfect wonderful selves and flip the switch of our innate wisdom, compassion, and determination to NEVER GIVE UP until we've won in our challenge. It's a unique kind of revolution… it's a Human Revolution… and our battle is with our own darkness, but the light switch has always been there, we're simply gifted the owner's manual.

Like I mentioned in the very beginning, we're all snowflakes… no two are alike, our circumstances vary widely due to our own unique karma, whether it be good, bad, or indifferent. But when we take on this humanistic practice of turning the poisonous aspects of our lives into a happiness we could not otherwise imagine, is when we truly begin to live.

I marvel at my web. I marvel at the strength of the thread it weaves. I marvel at the thought that this is only the tip of the iceberg. I marvel at the fact that my life has some incredible, magnetic ability to gather from all corners of the planet and link these karmic relationships. I look forward with anticipation and excitement to the next chapter which patiently lies in wait.

I have built a life of tremendous fortune because of the swamp I've muddled around in for eons. Because that swamp was filled with such diversity of pain, it has afforded me an incomparable opportunity to encourage and inspire so many others to find their own courage, strength, and determination to stand up and fight for their own happiness! I also have the wisdom to know that it ain't over until I take my last breath. And right now, my breathing is just fine!

PUDDLE JUMPERS

Love your mission with a passion; there is nothing more beautiful.

———————

Auguste Rodin

THE KISS

It seems like my entire childhood took place in 1959 when I was in the fourth grade.

Randy moved catty-corner to us that year. He was that dreamy older man… he was a sixth grader… and he had a built-in swimming pool… and we lived in the desert, so that made him the catch of our elementary school.

At the first sign of summer, Randy invited me over to go swimming… that invitation expanded into a daily routine. One day, I wanted to test my endurance by seeing how far I could swim underwater without coming up for air. As I approached the other end of the pool, I was met head on by a sweet set of lips. Those were condor wings pounding in my stomach, not butterflies.

That was the second time I was kissed underwater by a cute fella. The first time I was five years old. We had a little blowup circular kiddie pool in our backyard. My neighbor, Jerry, did the same thing in our little pool as we swam with our faces in the six inches of water in opposite directions until our lips collided. That was my first kiss and I know it was an "on purpose." Even back then I liked it, but those were most definitely tiny butterflies, but butterflies, nonetheless.

Anyway, Randy and I remained good friends throughout high school, but as with all new fledgling adults, our lives took separate paths and we never saw each other again.

One day in 1977 (that would make me 27), the man I was dating at the time took me to the famous Brown Derby Restaurant in Hollywood for lunch. It was my first and only time there. Being the romantic that I am, and a big fan of that old Silver Screen, I was mesmerized by the ghosts who graced those tables of times past.

Sitting at the table right next to us was a man who looked so familiar. He was obviously experiencing the same out of context moment as we both inconspicuously continued glancing over at each other trying to drum up the familiarity. Simultaneously, we got up from our seats… "Debbie?" and then "Randy?" He was in a business luncheon, so we cut it short after a few warm hugs and an exchange of phone numbers that neither of us would ever use. During our short encounter, he told me he was a record producer for a major label in Nashville.

Several jobs and locations later, as in the early 1990s, I was working as a legal secretary for a small law firm in Hollywood. One of the attorneys in the office was a music attorney. When our receptionist had to step out for lunch or a break, the three secretaries in the office would rotate turns answering the phones. One day when it was my turn, a call came in,

Me: "Mr. S's office."

Caller: "Is Mr. S there?"

Me: "He is out of the office at the moment, may I take a message?"

Caller: "Yes, tell him Randy from Nashville called."

Me: "May I have your last name and phone number?"

Caller: "Oh, sorry, Randy T, and my number is…"

Me: "Randy T?"

Caller: "Yes."

Me: "Randy T., as in Lancaster, California?"

Caller: "Why, yes."

Me: "Randy T., the best underwater kisser ever?"

Caller: "Oh, my god… Debbie, is that you?"

He was running the largest music publishing company in the country. Over the next several years, he would call when I would just happen to be on phone relief duty. I haven't spoken to him since I left that firm, but we've got time.

JUDY, JUDY, JUDY

From 1983 through 1985, I worked for a boutique law firm in Beverly Hills. My office manager's name was Judy. There were two partners (who co-owned the firm) along with three associate attorneys (who did all the work for them). I worked for one of the associates, Trish, who sadly had gone through half a dozen secretaries in one year before I jumped on board. She was a tough nut which made it difficult for most people to work for her. But somehow, we got along just fine.

One of the cases we were working on was a huge class action real estate litigation with dozens of plaintiffs and defendants spread out all over the country. One day, Trish was out of the office in deposition and my instructions were to contact all the parties to coordinate dates for multitudes of future depositions. I was on the phone all day long attempting to achieve that task.

At the end of the day, Judy called me into her office. Her eyes were all red and puffy; it was apparent she had been crying. Apprehensively, she said that one of the partners had fired me because every time he walked by my desk I was on the phone. She tried to explain to him why I was on the phone all day, but he wasn't interested in hearing an explanation. I was nearly eight months pregnant with my second child at the time.

Early the next morning, Trish called, a bit miffed that I wasn't at my desk. I told her I no longer had a desk. She was flabbergasted! She told me not to worry about it, and that she would go and have a talk with the boss. We hung up and a short time later she called me back. She was crying as well. She told him I had been on the phone all day at her instruction to organize and coordinate dozens of deposition dates with dozens of parties. He was not interested in listening. That's the end of that part of the story.

My fourth husband and I left the Los Angeles area in early 1987 to open a Stride Rite Children's Shoe Store in the Antelope Valley. While he ran the store, I studied real estate and became an agent. When the real estate market crashed in 1990, we lost everything, and came far too close for comfort to living in our car with two kids.

I knew if I could just get close enough to Los Angeles, I could find a job in a law firm, and we'd be able to pull ourselves back up.

I found the number for a legal placement agency and spoke with the owner, Jan. She sent me on an interview to a three-attorney firm in Hollywood. When I arrived for the interview, I was greeted by Wendy and David, who were two of the three associates in the Beverly Hills firm where I had been fired four years earlier.

Interestingly, the job order for this position was not Jan's, it belonged to another agency in Santa Monica. Jan had just heard about it and thought I might be a good fit and the agent in Santa Monica who had the listing knew nothing about me.

Wendy and David hired me on the spot. We had been quite friendly at the Beverly Hills firm, and they were confident in my work ethics, professionalism, and sense of humor. They wanted to know if I was surprised that Judy (my former office manager) now owned her own placement agency. I had no idea what they were talking about. So, yes, when they explained to me that I landed in their office because of Judy (indirectly), it undeniably made for an interesting topic on synchronicity. I worked with them for several years and then in December of 1996, I moved on to a firm in the Twin Towers in Century City.

One day while I was out on the plaza in Century City having lunch, I saw Judy walking by. She and her business partner had been in a promotional meeting in one of the firms. There was plenty of room at my table, so they joined me. Naturally they wanted to know where I was working. When I told them, Judy's partner said she knew two of the attorneys in my office quite well; they had gone to law school with her son and the three of them had remained close friends. The firm where I worked occupied three and half floors. Realistically, you could work in that firm for a long time and never happen upon a good portion of fellow co-workers. When I asked who the two attorneys were, lo and behold, they were the two attorneys I was supporting.

Months later, Donna, one of my co-workers, and I were looking for a place to sit on the plaza to have lunch when I spied Judy again. As Donna and I took a seat with Judy, the two of them realized they were long lost friends from high school back in the early 1960s.

Before I wrap up this segment… just a little food for thought… there are 3.999 million people in Los Angeles, and of the 3.999 million people, over 25,000 of them are attorneys. With that being said, the odds of just one of these Judy stories happening are one in 25,000. I am now up to four with her that I'm aware of.

MRS. BEASLEY

I moved to a little wood-frame cottage at the top of the hill on Coronado Street in a historic section of Los Angeles known as Echo Park in 1976. The property was about an acre of land that housed two large Spanish duplexes, one at the street level and one at the far rear of the property. In the middle of the two sat my little cottage.

My cousin Jeri and her husband lived in the front unit of the rear duplex. A woman named Sandy lived in the unit behind them. It was a lovely tree-filled, hilly area with tons of historic nostalgia, along with a communal garden. I lived there less than a year when I moved on to my next adventure.

Nearly twenty years later, in 1991, I was the acting office manager and legal secretary for Wendy and David in the Hollywood firm. One of our secretaries was leaving to further her education, so it was my job to scout for her replacement. I had interviewed an over-abundance of candidates, most of whom would be just fine. When my last and final prospect arrived, I chuckled to myself at how much she reminded me of Mrs. Beasley… a lovable character from an old television series *Family Affair.* As I reviewed her resume, I remarked that her address was on Coronado Street, and mentioned that I had lived on Coronado Street many years before. She asked me where I had lived, but I was only able to describe the property as I had long ago forgotten the address. I told her that when I lived there, my cousin and her husband lived in the duplex behind my little house. She said it sounded just like where she lived. Then she went on to say that her sister, Sandy, had lived in the rear duplex for years, and that when she moved, Mrs. Beasley took over her space, then added that her neighbors in the unit in front of her had been Jeri and John. Well, of course they were.

GRAMMY AWARD WINNER

When I worked for the law firm in Hollywood, we lived in Canyon Country, which was about 30 miles away.

One of the attorneys in our office, Al, was a music attorney. He was responsible for the production of the Grammy Awards one year. A lot of excitement was brewing in the office leading up to that event as we all looked forward to watching it.

My daughter was in junior high school, and she had a boyfriend named Ben. Ben was in a youth choir with his church and that was all we knew about Ben.

The evening of the Grammy's arrived and with popcorn in hand, my little family gathered around the tube to spectate. One of the performances was an amazingly talented youth choir. My daughter caught a closeup glimpse of the performers and spied Ben, right there on that stage. Well, that certainly knocked our enthusiasm up a notch. Then… the award presentation… Ben's choir won the Grammy in their category! He had his own trophy!

Bright and early the next morning at work, Al was ecstatic! His clients had WON! Al represented Ben and the choir. Who knew?

RETURN TO CAMELOT

For the two years before we moved to Canyon Country, California, we lived in a beautiful, rural mountain community called Tehachapi, which is about two hours north of Canyon Country. While we lived in Tehachapi, I practiced Buddhism with a tiny local group. One elderly couple I practiced with spoke often about their children and grandchildren who lived in Simi Valley. One of their granddaughters was named Monique.

Bear with me as I do a little stage setting.

After living in Canyon Country for a couple of years, we moved into our second house which was on Camelot Court… the wonderful house where we lived during the Northridge earthquake. We had been hit extremely hard and I was terrified to stay in that house. My Buddhist altar (called a butsudan), among so many other things, had been badly damaged, and as I'm not a carpenter, I stored it in the garage. About six months later we bought a house another mile down the road, and I left the butsudan in the garage.

My daughter was in high school at the time and was active with the drama department. She would sometimes mention student's names, one being Monique, but I never paid much attention to it. After we moved into our new house, my daughter had told me that her friend Monique had moved into our old one.

One evening while I was attending a Buddhist meeting, a woman I had not seen before shared an experience regarding how she and her husband had separated, and that she and her daughters had recently moved from Simi Valley to Canyon Country. Having left everything behind, she no longer had a butsudan, but lo and behold, there in her new garage, was a butsudan. She said her father was a carpenter and had been able to beautifully restore it. Obviously, it was my old house, my old butsudan, and her carpenter father happened to be my old friend and neighbor in Tehachapi.

OH, HOW LIVELY

In 1990, as the country faced a critical recession, my husband John and I lost our Stride Rite Children's Shoe Store in Lancaster, and my real estate business went under. We came very close to living in our cars with two children.

One of my sisters lived in Canyon Country and she knew of a house for rent around the corner from them. I had never received child support from my daughter's father, but he caught wind of our struggle, and without my asking him for help, he showed up with a year's worth of child support which enabled us to move into that little house. Shortly after we settled in, a single woman and her two children moved next door from Colorado. We became friends as did our kids. On the Fourth of July we took our families to the local community college for the festivities and fireworks. A stage was set up on the football field where bands played all day. People were camped all around the field with picnic gear and outdoor games.

At one point, my neighbor noticed a man on the stage who she said was an old friend of hers from Colorado. She was incredibly excited to see him and made a mad dash for the stage. His appearance was quite distinct as he was albino.

A year later, we moved into a bigger house a few miles down the road where my new neighbor and I became fast friends. Our sons were the same age and became inseparable. During the Christmas holiday she invited my family to come see her perform at her church's Christmas pageant. In her earlier life she had been a professional singer, and I was excited to have the opportunity to see her perform. Oddly, her singing partner was the albino man who was my last neighbor's friend from Colorado.

Oh, it doesn't end there…

About two years later, we bought a house another mile down the road. As we were unloading the moving truck, our new neighbor came to offer the helping hands of his teenage boys. We struck up a conversation and he told me he was a local attorney. I told him I was a commuting legal secretary and gave him a copy of my resume with a plug that if he ever heard of a local attorney in need of a secretary who would pay Los Angeles wages, please give them my name.

Many months later, I had a terrible falling out with one of the attorneys in the office where I worked, and I did the unthinkable… I quit my job… without something else lined up, and I was essentially the primary source of income for my family. I waited until I got home to tell my husband I had quit. As I walked in the house, and before I could break the news, my husband told me that our neighbor had just stopped by to let me know a friend of his was looking for a secretary. What timing!

I made the call first thing in the morning and the next day I went in for an interview with Mr. Lively. As I walked into his office, I could not believe my eyes… he was a dead ringer for the albino friend of my past two neighbors… he was his brother. I was hired on the spot complete with Los Angeles wages.

I had not been to a Buddhist meeting for a few years, and I decided it was time to find a group in my new area. As I approached the meeting house for the first time, I saw an old chanting buddy, Howard, standing by the front door. He and I had practiced Buddhism together in Los Angeles 20 years prior. We played a bit of catch up and I told him I was working in a law office in Valencia. He told me he had a niece who worked in a law office in Valencia. He asked me where I worked, and I told him. He said that was where his niece worked. Aside from me, there was Mr. Lively, one associate attorney and the bookkeeper who was Howard's niece.

MELODY... MUSIC TO MY EARS

In 1994, the Hollywood firm where I worked moved their offices to Century City. My husband and I had bought a house in Canyon Country, which is about 34 miles away. Melody was one of my new neighbors, another one who had moved to California from Colorado (no connection… to my knowledge). She and I became early morning walking buddies. On our walks, we talked about everything under the sun. Oftentimes she shared stories about her best friend, Rochelle. They had been friends since their college days in Denver. Melody was in her early 50's at the time, so it had been decades since they lived near one another, but they had maintained their friendship despite the distance.

After some months, Melody found herself in desperate need of a job. The company she had been working for moved out of state and the job market in her field had become very tight. She specialized in corporate computer networking and installation of appropriate work-related programs along with employee and management training. After being on the hunt for longer than she could afford, I told her our receptionist was leaving and offered her the position, even if only as a temporary remedy. She jumped on it and came in to meet the attorneys the following morning. One of the three attorneys, quite surprisingly, was Rochelle's brother, who Melody had known for over 30 years. Slam dunk!

INSTANT MESSAGE

I bought my first computer on May 2, 1998. My co-worker and friend Diane (Howard's niece), along with her two kids helped me select it and set it up. They signed me up for America Online and walked me through some of the space-aged options that were available. It was all Greek to me. That evening was my first online adventure. Thanks to my friend, Phyllis, I found my way to a Jewish chatroom where I met a man from Albuquerque, New Mexico. I had a great time chatting up a storm and meeting people from all around the country. A few days after meeting Mr. Albuquerque, he sent me an Instant Message so we could talk privately. Our conversations continued every evening.

In August of 1997, my good friend Pat moved from Los Angeles to South Carolina. We continued our friendship via emails from work, almost daily.

Flash forward to Mr. Albuquerque and Instant Messaging… one day, Pat told me she was going to visit her mother who lived in Albuquerque. I told her all about this man I had been talking to on the Internet. I told her he was a high school teacher in Albuquerque and invited her to play a schoolgirl game with me by going to his school library, copying his picture out of the yearbook, and sending it to me so I could see what he looked like. Naturally, she said she'd be delighted to. After asking what high school he taught in, it turned out that her nephew not only attended that school but was in Mr. Albuquerque's class. How many schools do you suppose are in the United States? I looked it up… 62,000 SECONDARY SCHOOLS! How many students do you suspect occupy those schools?

ONLINE DATING

I started working for a boutique law firm in Century City in the mid-1990s. The office mommy was Rosalie. She had been with the firm since its inception when they had a handful of attorneys. When I began working for them, they were up to 30, and by the time I left the firm in 2004 to move to Alaska, they occupied three and a half floors in the Twin Towers in Century City.

Rosalie and her husband were avid square dancers. Not so unusual I suppose unless you're Jewish, and they were. I can't imagine there are many Jewish square dancers. Anyway, they traveled all over the place to dance. Rosalie was a hoot. She wound down her career and came into the office only a couple of times a month to handle the office social calendar. Whenever she was in the office, she made it a point to come and share her latest dirty jokes with me.

For a year or so, she was dropping hints about a good friend of theirs who she thought would be a nice fit for me. I had already been through the ringer with four marriages. The absolute last thing I was interested in was a relationship. That would also include dating… NOPE… no thank you!

Much to everyone's heartfelt dismay, Rosalie passed away suddenly.

In 2001, after being single for many years, I thought I'd dip my toe in the water and I put a profile on a Jewish dating site.

One of the men who contacted me seemed like a decent and interesting man. Our phone conversation was going well when I asked what kinds of things he enjoyed doing. He said, "Well, I know it may sound odd, but I enjoy square dancing." Hmmmmmm. Naturally, the next thing out of my mouth was, "Do you know Rosalie?" Of course, he did. They had been friends forever. He said she was a gem… when she entered a room it lit up. Then he went on to say that she used to tell him about a woman she worked with that she wanted him to meet. Then he asked me how I knew Rosalie. I told him I was the woman she wanted him to meet. There were approximately 25 million profiles on dating sites at that time.

∧∧∧

Then there was a conversation with another fella and the topic of synchronicity came up. He asked me what that meant, and I began sharing my tale about Charles Byrd in Hershey, PA, when I bought one of my auntie's albums on eBay. He interrupted me to ask who my aunt was, and since it wasn't pertinent to the story of synchronicity, I told him she was before his time and he probably wouldn't know who she was anyway, so I continued. He interrupted again to ask, and I politely said her name was Gogi Grant. He said, "You're kidding me! My uncle is Herb Newman." Okay… didn't ring a bell. "Who is Herb Newman?" He replied, "Herb Newman wrote *The Wayward Wind*," the hit song my aunt recorded that knocked Elvis off the charts in 1956.

ELLEN AND THE ELEVATOR

For months Ellen and I frequented the same elevator in my office building. Mind you, I was in one of the Century City Twin Towers, which exhibited twelve elevators.

At some point, I remarked that I thought she looked familiar, but neither of us could pinpoint anything. One day, I was out on the plaza when we ended up sharing a table for lunch. During our conversation, she told me she worked for HBO. I told her one of my cousins had some kind of a deal going on with them. She said his name sounded familiar. As the conversation progressed, she said she had worked for Castlerock prior to coming to HBO. I told her my cousin worked in their offices. She said that was where she had heard that name. She told me she had grown up on the Westside and I asked her if she knew any Arinsbergs (my mom's very large family). She said she didn't. I asked her where she currently lived, and she told me she lived on Stanley Avenue. I told her I lived on Stanley Avenue for 11 years. Then she began talking about her moonlighting… she was a DJ on Friday nights for a blues station. I asked her if she knew Keb Mo, and of course she did. Not only was she familiar with him as an artist, but she had recently interviewed him on the air. I said he had been a close friend of mine and my family. He worked in my uncle's flower shop, he had a romance with my cousin, he was the first one to come and see my daughter after her birth, and he sang at one of my weddings. Then I asked her if she was familiar with Gogi Grant. Most definitely she was… her mother was my Auntie Gogi's tennis partner.

AFTER-WORDS

Just as flowers open up and bear fruit, just as the moon appears and invariably grows full, just as a lamp becomes brighter when oil is added, and just as plants and trees flourish with rain, so will human beings never fail to prosper when they make good causes.

———

Nichiren Daishonin

THIRST QUENCHERS

I hope my journey has inspired a curiosity to discover the magnificence of your life through this wonderful, hope-filled humanistic philosophy.

I've selected a diversity of great reads I think you'll find captivating. To locate a discussion group in your area, feel free to contact the World Culture Center, explore the SGI-USA website listed below, or shoot me an email.

The Winning Life: An Introduction to Buddhist Practice
World Tribune Press 2016

The Buddha in Your Mirror: Practical Buddhism and the Search for Self
Woody Hochswender, Greg Martin & Ted Marino. Middleway Press 2001

A Baptist Preacher's Buddhist Teacher: How My Interfaith Journey with Daisaku Ikeda Made Me a Better Christian Lawrence Edward Carter, Sr., Dean of the Martin Luther King Jr. International Chapel. Middleway Press 2018

Choose Hope: Your Role in Waging Peace in the Nuclear Age David Krieger & Daisaku Ikeda. Middleway Press 2002

Happiness Becomes You: A Guide to Changing Your Life for Good
Tina Turner. Atria Books 2020

Possibilities, Herbie Hancock and Lisa Dickey Penguin Books 2015

AUDIO VISUALS

Our Shared Humanity Soka Gakkai Buddhist Movement
[Video] YouTube. https://youtu.be/y3xOf-jXJSY

Buddhability.com

Mahindra Humanities Center, Harvard University
Herbie Hancock: Buddhism and Creativity
[Video] YouTube. https://youtu.be/xSFMkJQKigk

FOR MORE INFORMATION

World Culture Center Soka Gakkai International
525 Wilshire Boulevard
Santa Monica, CA 90401

(310) 260-8900
www.sgi-usa.org or sgi-usa app

CONTACT THE AUTHOR

Deborah Favorite
synchronicityisnocoincidence@gmail.com

Author Bio

Deborah Favorite's life has been an overflowing reservoir of mindboggling synchronicities. Her stories are sensitive and humorous and are genuine tales of triumph over tragedy.

Although she had glimpses of synchronistic episodes since her early youth, the frequency of these remarkable manifestations became abundant when she began the hope-filled Buddhist practice of chanting Nam-myoho-renge-kyo in 1975. That's when her life transformed, and she began to soar.

Changing hats certainly has been her signature style as she refers to herself as a Jack(ess) of many trades. She was a Beverly Hills hairstylist, a back office medical assistant, and a litigation secretary working on some of the country's most notorious civil litigation cases. She was a realtor, a business owner, and a human/civil rights activist and organizer. But most importantly she is the mother of two stellar young adults and three Fab-A-Lus grandsons.

She authored a children's book for ages 3 to 103 titled *The Tush People* by Debbie and Uncle Norm, along with an animated version that can be viewed on her YouTube Channel, Deborah Favorite's Videos.

This memoir has been a reflective work through sweat and tears… with a heaping portion of love. Deborah's wish is that her captivating stories will bewilder her audience, spurring them on to uncover the gateway to their own magical portals.